JAZZ

FOR BEGINNERS

BY RON DAVID
ILLUSTRATED BY VANESSA HOLLEY

WRITERS AND READERS PUBLISHING, INC.
P.O. Box 461, Village Station
New York, NY 10014

Writers and Readers Limited
9 Cynthia Street
London N1 9JF
England

A Writers and Readers Documentary Comic Book Copyright © 1995

ISBN # 0-86316-165-0

1 2 3 4 5 6 7 8 9 0

Manufactured in the United States of America

Contents

Publisher's Dedication:

I dedicate this book to my three children, Shoshannah, Benjamin and Elisha, and my two grandchildren, Nathaniel and Robin. So that they can remember our Mother Africa and this great black music. To Rob for all the good Jazz-talking, mother-thumping moments, your wise and truthful advice, your humanity and deep pockets. I know wherever you are, you're wailing with the best.

J.B. -- Think about you always.

-- Glenn Thompson

John Coltrane
where have you gone?
we can still feel your sax dragging its tongue
along the carpet they call alabama
sweet sweet alabama
land of the cotton
why are those four little black girls
still bleeding in your belly?
-- "altar for four" from *recognize* by Kevin Powell

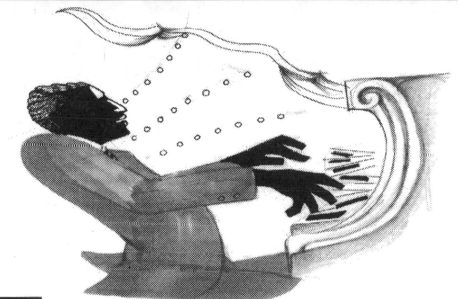

Introduction

WHAT'S so SPECIAL ABOUT JAZZ?
DOES IT REACH BEYOND MUSIC
...OR ONLY SEEM TO?

I know that Jazz has been called "America's only original art form," and I realize that in 100 years it's covered pretty much the same ground (and painted itself into the same corner) that it took European classical music 1000 years to do? And that the music itself is strong and beautiful.

But aside from that (!)...is there anything special about it? Does it really reach beyond music ... or merely seem to?

I decided it was a dumb line of questioning—I loved the music so much that I was trying to inflate its importance.

Then, halfway through writing this book, it hit me...

Listening to a great Jazz solo is the closest I will ever get to being in a room with Einstein when he flashes on his Theory of Relativity or with Sir Isaac Newton when he realizes that the apple falls down, not up. (Or that if you grind up some figs...)

"He never stopped surprising himself."
--Alice Coltrane, describing her husband, John.

Listening to a great Jazz solo, not only am I getting Charlie Parker's Theory of Relativity, but I am there with him at the moment he is creating it.

Great works of Art or Science are the result of an outrageously creative act. But a great Jazz solo is the creative act itself:

"Sometimes I'm able to step outside myself and hear what I'm playing. The ideas just flow. The horn and I become one."
-- Sonny Rollins

That moment when the ideas just flow, when you and the horn
(or pen or basketball)
become one. . .

... if we hang around it long enough, maybe it'll rub off.

What Is Jazz?

The closest I can get to answering that is to say that jazz is playing what you feel. All Jazz musicians express themselves through their instruments; they express the types of persons they are... there is no way they can subterfuge their feelings."

-- Jo Jones, drummer (& cymbal thrower) in Count Basie's band, from "*Jazz Is*" by Nat Hentoff.

JAZZ IS..."a musical form, often improvisational, developed by Afro-Americans and influenced by both European harmonic structure and African rhythmic complexity."

-- Encyclo - *whitebread* - pedia Britannica

JAZZ IS... "The music, yearning like a God in pain."

-- John Keats —From "*The Eve of St. Agnes*" (1820).

JAZZ IS... "a nigger word that white folks dropped on us."

-- From the ever cheerful Miles Davis.

JAZZ IS... "Then I had an attack, broke out in cold sweat, felt faint. Billie [Holiday] noticed and told me to go outside;

she'd watch my horn. She said she'd watched Pres' [Lester Young] horn for him when he had to go out. When I came back she was singing 'Detour Ahead.' I listened to the anguish in her voice and the lyrics seemed to be about my own problems. I started to cry."

> -- Sam Rivers, reedman, teacher, composer, from *New York Jazz Museum* booklet

Jazz is..."syncopated music that emerged in America from a tangled mass of roots in African music plus European classical, tin-pan alley and folk."

> --from *"JAZZ—The Essential CD Guide"* by Martin Gayford.

Paul Gordon

JAZZ IS...a passionate fusion of African, European and American music.

QUESTION

How did this Passionate Fusion come about?

Statements about Jazz's origins (true, false, or ridiculous) reverberate with racial implications that invariably piss off one side or the other. This is a book on music, not history, politics, or race. Out of respect for people who want the music, period, I will avoid the bloody part of Jazz's origin here.

Out of respect for the truth, I will face it head-on in the last chapter: "What Is Jazz -- Part 2."

How Did Jazz Begin?

The slave trade forcibly took hundreds of thousands of Yorubas, Dahomeans, Senegalese, and Ashantis—each with its own musical tradition—from Africa and dumped them into the cotton and tobacco plantations of the Carribean and the Americas.

Just as the traditions of the slaves varied, so did those of the slave owners. The Catholics — Spanish, French, Portugese — generally left West African culture more intact than British Protestants, who were so offended by the dancing and drumming that they banned it.

HOW DID JAZZ BEGIN?
THERE IS NO EXACT ANSWER.

It started with the African captives' determination to keep their own culture alive, even if they had to disguise it. Like: the slaves played drums for St. Patrick's Day, merging the rituals of Catholicism and West Africa by dressing one religion in the gowns of another!

"... with the moans and groans of the people in the cottonfields. Before it got the name of soul, men were sellin' watermelons and vegetables on a wagon drawn by a mule, hollerin' 'watermellllon!' with a cry in their voices. And the men on the railroad track layin' crossties—everytime they hit the hammer it was with a sad feelin, but with a beat. And the Baptist preacher—he the one who had the soul—he give out the meter, a long and short meter, and the old mothers of the church would reply. This musical thing has been here since America been here. This is trial and tribulation music."

-- Mahalia Jackson, Time magazine, June 28, 1968

As early as the 1770s, a preacher known as Black Harry became famous for his fiery sermons. Harry juiced up the droopy psalms with a little rhythmic beat, plus the exciting sliding pitch common to African languages, and he got the congregation involved with a technique called "lining out"...

Lining out was a British church practice (designed to deal with churchgoers who couldn't read the prayer book) in which the congregation had to repeat the preacher's words every couple lines...which was a lot like the African "call-&-response" pattern:

Call-&-response—you say it, I repeat it—had been used by African musicians for hundreds of years. You can hear it in gospel music and in the riffs (riff = short melody or rhythmic phrase that's repeated) traded between sections in big band Jazz or the soloists in small group Jazz.

It started with the difference between African and European musical traditions.

"Those African slaves had a musical tradition as sophisticated as that of the West, but one which had developed in a diametrically opposite direction. Where Europeans had focused on harmony ... the Africans had focused on ... rhythm."

-- "JAZZ—the Essential CD Guide" by Martin Gayford.

The African Melody Line is also different from the West's. When the African five-note (pentatonic) scale met the European seven-note (diatonic) scale, all hell broke loose!

When African music collided with the music of the European and American church, army, and concert hall—expressive pre-Jazz hybrids evolved.

The most important hybrids were **Blues** and **Ragtime**:

Blues: The song form central to Jazz (and Rock 'n Roll) developed in the late 19th century from a mix of African field hollers and Christian hymns.

Ragtime: Syncopated, European style of piano music that took its formal structure from the march but was played with African rhythmic undertones.

THE SAD TRUTH

There were plantation brass bands as early as 1835. Touring minstrel troupes were singing and playing early versions of the blues by the 1840s. Ragtime, the herky jerky forerunner of Jazz, was fully developed in the 1890s. But nobody knows when all those pretty approximations became the real thing. Nobody knows exactly when Jazz emerged. (Or who "emerged" it.)

We don't know exactly when or who, but we do know where.

(Sort of.)

> "Jazz began in New Orleans and worked its way up the river to Chicago," is the announcement most investigators...are apt to make when dealing with the vague subject of Jazz and its origins. And while that is certainly a rational explanation...it is more than likely untrue. Jazz...could no more have begun in one area of the country than could Blues.
>
> Even though New Orleans cannot be thought of with any historical veracity as the "birthplace of Jazz," there has been so much investigation of the Jazz and earlier music characteristic there in the first part of the twentieth century, that from New Orleans conclusions may be drawn concerning...the creation of Jazz."
> -- From "BLUES PEOPLE" by Leroi Jones [aka Amiri Baraka]

1900-1920
New Orleans

New Orleans was -- and is -- an exceptional city. Originally a French settlement, and one of the great melting pots of the 19th century, it didn't become part of the USA until the Louisiana Purchase of 1803, so it retained its European character longer than any other major American city.

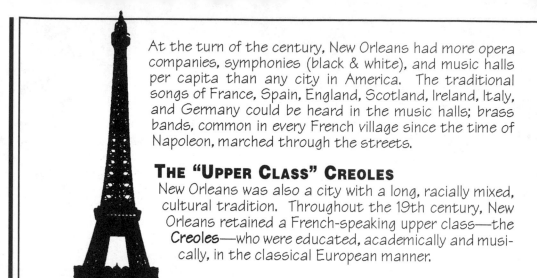

At the turn of the century, New Orleans had more opera companies, symphonies (black & white), and music halls per capita than any city in America. The traditional songs of France, Spain, England, Scotland, Ireland, Italy, and Germany could be heard in the music halls; brass bands, common in every French village since the time of Napoleon, marched through the streets.

THE "UPPER CLASS" CREOLES

New Orleans was also a city with a long, racially mixed, cultural tradition. Throughout the 19th century, New Orleans retained a French-speaking upper class—the **Creoles**—who were educated, academically and musically, in the classical European manner.

> **Creole** : People of mixed race initially French and Spanish, ultimately of each and/or Spanish and African descent.

For the Creoles, there was little or no discrimination during the early 19th century.

BLACK FREEMEN & BLACK SLAVES

At the beginning of the 1800s, the population of New Orleans was roughly half black and half white. About half of the blacks were considered "working class." The others were slaves. Captive Africans continued to be brought into New Orleans throughout the 19th century. Congo Square was the officially tolerated "headquarters" of their music and dance.

As if to compensate for the freedom that had been ripped from their lives, the slaves met in Congo Square, and in nightly explosions of creativity, began combining European musical instruments with African instruments and singing African call-&-response patterns in Creole and blending North European jigs and square dances into African dances. When they mixed Catholicism with African ancestor worship—talk about fusion!—they called it "voodoo."

(Hold that thought: Voodoo'll be back. First, let's hear...)

...AN OLD FAMILIAR SONG

After the U.S. acquired New Orleans in the Louisiana Purchase, American settlers came south in increasing numbers. As Whites poured into the city, working-class blacks were jammed out of the good neighbor- hoods and decent jobs.

By 1890, racial discrimination had broadened its retarded hate-list to include the Creoles. Sophisticated Creole musicians, forced to move uptown to what was rapidly becoming a ghet- to, suddenly found them- selves playing alongside homemade black musicians who made up most of the music as they went along.

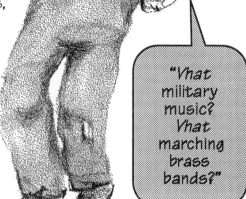

"Vhat military music? Vhat marching brass bands?"

Not only that: Voodoo had permeated the uptown black areas and brought with it a music of such radically elo- quent rhythms that they kept disrupting the nice orderly military music that the marching brass bands played.

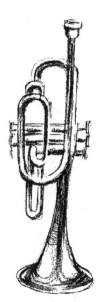

ART IMITATES LIFE (BUT THEY BOTH FOLLOW COMMERCE)

One of the weirder results of the Civil War was that, when it ended, there was suddenly a plentiful supply of cheap military marching band instruments. (On paper, the Civil War freed the slaves; in real life it gave them trumpets.)

Therefore: the music of late 19th century New Orleans, along with the rest of America, was domi- nated by brass bands. Brass bands played for parades, dances, riverboat trips, and above all... funerals.

THE SAINTS GO MARCHING

For the black populace, virtually all of whom had been recently stolen from West African cultures that respected their dead, devoting music and passion to honor the death of a loved one was a reminder of home. To the displaced West Africans, their funeral marching brass bands breaking out all over New Orleans weren't about inventing some clever new music called Jazz. They had been deprived of honoring their dead in Africa and on the terrible ships during the crossing, so they would honor their dead, here, now, while pretending—no, not pretending—while *honoring* another's dead (or perhaps their own).

There weren't faking those impassioned graveside ceremonies. And there are few things in life more real than those raucous, hell-raising, life-affirming, marching band journeys back into town.

New Orleans Jazz classics like "When the Saints Go Marching In" were originally funeral band tunes.

STORYVILLE

Then, as now, New Orleans jumped on any excuse to party, either standing up or lying down. In 1897, New Orleans created a legal red-light district—Storyville. The sporting houses of Storyville were a good source of work for slick young "pianists" like Jelly Roll Morton. (See Jelly Roll's bio in Part II.)

The streets of Storyville—and much of New Orleans—were filled with big, noisy, walking parties (Mardi gras, picnics, dances, funerals) disguised as parades. A proper, hell-raising New Orleans parade required music. The music was handled mainly by two groups: working-class blacks and Creoles of color.

It is in the interaction between blacks & Creoles that most scholars see the origin of Jazz.

The Creoles, depending upon which way the winds of criticism were blowing, were considered part of New Orlean's middle class, so many of them were well-educated in the European tradition, including composing and performing European classical music. The French-educated Creoles read Western music and played instruments with "classical" technique, so they were more likely to be the instrumental virtuosos of early Jazz. **Jelly Roll Morton** and **Sidney Bechet,** two of Jazz's early giants, were Creoles. Black musicians, on the other hand, generally couldn't read music, but they seldom had trouble playing it by ear. Not only that -- the rhythmic flair they'd inherited from their ancestors in Africa gave them an edge that the Creoles lacked.

Sidney Bechet

J. R. Morton

The black musicians played the instruments of the Creole bands, but at moments of emotional climax, they bent and roughened their instrumental sounds the way a gospel or blues singer would.

Take the technical skill of the Creole players, wrestle it in with the earthy, bluesy music of the Black musicians, and toss 'em all into a New Orleans street band. (Thump, thump) The street bands were everywhere. They played in the streets or inside buildings or on the backs of carts and the gleeful thump of the drum was perfect for...something.

* **Author's note:** That theory strikes me as a scholarly version of "*all Blacks have rhythm.*" But it is the Wisdom of the Day among jazz scholars and, astonishingly, it seems to be favored even more by Black jazz writers & musicians than by white ones!

THE STREET BANDS

The classic New Orleans instruments were cornet, clarinet, trombone, tuba, bass, drums, banjo and, guitar. The frontline instruments combined in a rough approximation of European counterpoint, but nothing was sacred, including the melody—the players spontaneously reworked it as they played.

The cornet was the dominating instrument. The clarinet would float above it, weaving a fluid, higher part. The trombones would fill in below it in the choppy New Orleans "tailgate" style (when a band played on a cart, the trombonist sat facing backward so his slide wouldn't knock everyone upside the head: "**tailgate**").

Rhythm instruments were drums, tuba, or string bass. Banjo was optional. They seldom used a piano because, unless you had George Foreman in your band, you couldn't very well take the thing to parades and picnics and marching funerals.

Marching bands weren't Jazz, but they were getting close. (Thump, thump.) They had to learn two things: how to **swing** and how to play the **Blues**.

THE BLUES

The Blues didn't take shape until the late 19th century, but their roots go back to the first work songs. Work songs were call-and-response, sung in time to the activity at hand: the leader would call out a line, and the workers would shout out a phrase to coincide with, say, the fall of a hammer. The songs were filled with **blue notes,** * the lines were often improvised, and the time was ragged...but they were the first crude version of the Blues.

THE BLUE NOTE: Jazz's ubiquitous blue note doesn't really exist on the European diatonic scale, but you can approximate it by flattening the third and seventh notes of that scale.

A blues scale

These "off pitch" sounding notes are common in African music.

Early Blues was casual—the singer/musician could pretty well do as he/she pleased—but by the end of 19th century, it had pretty well settled into the twelve-bar form we know today. Good thing it did; without it there'd be no such critter as Jazz. Why? Two reasons: one technical and one emotional (*or mythological*).

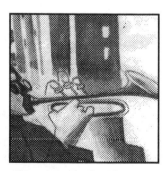
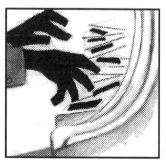

TECHNICAL: On the crudest technical level, Jazz's basic musical form is the twelve-bar Blues structure harmonized in the chord progression:

I-IV-I-V-I.

No twelve-bar Blues, no Jazz.

EMOTIONAL/MYTHOLOGICAL

Even more important, the Blues was the chronicle of black suffering and black strength, of black heroism and black humiliation and black spiritual rage and grace.

The Blues *songs* were, literally, the African-American *Iliad* and *Odyssey*

—the chronicle of a people's mythology—sung, not spoken, just like Homer's lovesongs to his people—but the Blues was written by *a people* instead of a person, and since you were still living in the country of your oppressor, the truth had to hide between the lines and the feeling had to be insides of the singer. (Maybe that's why Blues singers have such stature: *You better do a good job, chump, cause you're singing for all of us.*)

After 1900, Blues became more formalized. By 1910, it was a fully developed idiom with real honest-to-God written songs like W.C. Handy's "St. Louis Blues."

Jazz knew how to play the Blues. Now it had to learn how to **swing.**

Ragtime isn't Jazz. It has more in common with European marching band music and Polish polkas than it does with Jazz.

But it swung!

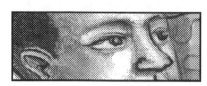

Sorry to be redundant, but we don't know exactly how, when, or where Ragtime started. What we do know is that it was created by Creole and black musicians, that a crude form of it started popping up around the 1870s, and that it took Europe and America by storm in the 1890s.

Ragtime was a technically complex piano music that adapted European light classics—especially marches, polkas, and Chopin!—and com-

bined them with a steady, marchlike, two-beat left hand, while the right hand doubled the tempo and put the accents between the strong beats of the left hand instead of on top of them...thus "ragging" (or syncopating) the time.

The "cross-rhythmic" approach of Ragtime echoed back to the music of Africa (and voodoo music!), but it also had precedents in Western classical music. But generally speaking ...

European music emphosizes the strong beats -- the 1st and 3rd:

HEP (right) LEFT (right)

Jazz emphasizes the weak beats, creating what classical and ragtime musicdudes call "syncopation," and Jazzdudes call "swing." (You haven't heard the last of swing.)

Scott Joplin

Ragtime was lively, spunky, uniquely American music with many fine players, including the great **Tom Turpin**, **Louis Chauvin**, and (if I may put the cart before the horse) the Michael Jordan of Ragtime—**Scott Joplin**. Scott Joplin was the son of a slave, a child prodigy, the greatest Ragtimer ever, world famous by the time he was 21...and died a sad, beaten man at age 47. (See his Bio in Part II of the book.)

For all its surface vitality, Ragtime was rigid music. Even so, it's jaunty, chugging beat, mingled with straight marching time (Thump, thump.) became an important undertow to the dynamic 1920s and 1930s Jazz piano style known as "stride" and to the early Jazz bands. As Pops (aka Louis Armstrong) used to say...

"Now You Has Jazz"

Charles "Buddy" Bolden is usually credited with leading the first real Jazz band. Buddy was a charismatic cornet player with a huge sound. He began playing band-style Ragtime with improvised embellishments in the late 1890s; by the turn of the century, Buddy's band was playing in a collective improvisational style. In 1907, Buddy Bolden was committed to an insane asylum, where he stayed for the last 24 years of his life. He never recorded.

THE ART OF **IMPROVISAION**

Many people think that Jazz is the only music that is improvised.

That is as false as George Washington's teeth.

Like most of the top musicians of his day—and like Jazz musicians of today—Bach was an expert at improvisation, making up music on the spot.

Sadly though, because music was often composed on the spot, it was not always preserved on paper.... So even though more than one thousand of Bach's compositions have survived, it is staggering to think of those we'll never hear.

Baroque music had its rules and structure...but there were often also whole sections of improvisatory "free" passages that a composer only suggested to the performer through the barest outline.... Classical musicians of today shy away from improvisation, but in the Baroque Era a performer had to be skilled at it.

-- From "CLASSICAL MUSIC FOR BEGINNERS"
by Stacy & Michael ynch.

THE ORIGINAL DIXIELAND WHITE GUYS

Many New Orleans bands had followed Buddy's lead and were beginning to play in a collective improvisational style. One of the groups that picked up on the new style called itself the Original Dixieland Jazz Band. In 1917 the ODJB appeared at a fashionable restaurant on New York's Columbus Circle. The music they played struck the customers as so weird that they had to be told they could dance to it.

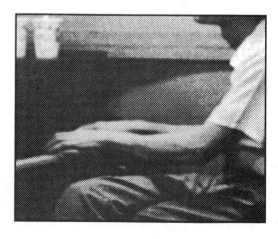

Two weeks later, the ODJB made the first ever Jazz recording, "Livery Stable Blues" and "Original Dixieland One-Step." It sold a million copies, and Jazz spread like the British Empire.

The Original Dixieland White Guys were decent musicians who played with enthusiasm—but they were not the originators of Jazz. Since no recordings of New Orleans Jazz were made until 1917, and none were made of black or Creole musicians until several years after that, we can only make reasonable guesses at what the real founders of Jazz sounded like.

By the time the new music of New Orleans first matured, it was already time to move.

The classics of "New Orleans" Jazz recorded in the 1920s by **Joe "King" Oliver** (1885-1938), **Ferdinand "Jelly Roll" Morton** (1890-1941), **Sidney Bechet** (1897-1959) and **Louis Armstrong** (1901-1971), were made in Chicago?

1920s
Chicago

When writer F. Scott Fitzgerald declared the 1920s "The Jazz Age," black jazz musicians who weren't even dead yet must have rolled over in their graves. (Fitzgerald's rich white kid, spoiled brat hedonism was an insult to the spirit of Jazz.)

To be fair: Fitzgerald was talking about a *feeling*, about the mood of America after the end of the-War-To-End-All-Wars and about the magic of radios and phonograph records and movies and cars. Suddenly, freedom wasn't a mere abstraction—you could actually pick up and *go*.

IN SEARCH OF A NEW LIFE

In 1900, 75% of America's black population lived in the rural South; fifty years later, that number had shrunk to 20%. These teeming migrations from the cotton fields and overt racism of the South to the factories (and less obvious racism) of the North followed America's thundering industrial economy.

Chicago in the 1920s meant the promise of a new life for the southern Black population, drawn to the city's expanding industries.

STORYVILLE NORTH

When New Orleans' fabled Storyville was closed down in 1917 (for being "detrimental to morale" during World War I—apparently they didn't notice that it was the *war,* not the HO-houses, that was "detrimental to morale"), its players, many of whom (Louis Armstrong, for one) had grown up in the sportin' houses, looked for a town just as tolerant of human frailty.

Chicago in the 1920s had more cabarets and dance joints than the entire South combined. And the money was a hell of a lot better. The bosses were a trifle unpredictable. (Chicago in the 1920s was under the spiritual guidance of gangsters.)

Not long after the ambitious migrants from the South arrived, Prohibition was voted in. The Prohibition laws that banned alcohol triggered an entire industry in bootleg liquor. In the illegal drinking clubs—called "speakeasies"—Jazz thrived. People looking for a drink wanted music to accompany it.

So the music obliged.

In 1918, **Joe "King" Oliver** left New Orleans and settled in Chicago, where he formed his famous Creole Band, which became a regular fixture at Lincoln Gardens on Chicago's South Side.

In 1922, Oliver sent for Louis Armstrong, the gifted young trumpeter he had taught in New Orleans ragtime bands. Armstrong had come a long way in the four years since his mentor had left the South:

"Louis Armstrong now had a melodic imagination extending beyond that of his teenage heroes, and one which could not be precisely tracked to any single influence more explicable than his own genius."
-- From _JAZZ_ by John Fordham

THE ART OF IMPROVISATION

When King Oliver brought Louis Armstrong into his band, he bent the rules of Jazz. For one thing, with the addition of Armstrong, the group had an unprecedented two cornet front line. The result was electrifying. Oliver was a fine trumpeter, but he never wandered far from the melody and beat.

Armstrong, on the other hand, was doubling the number of notes a mere mortal would squeeze into a bar. He'd shorten some notes, lengthen others, and loosen up the rhythm until the music began to ebb and flow instead of following the rigid rocking ragtime. He built his improvisations like songs within a song, and his trumpet sound glowed.

Historical Note: Before Louis Armstrong, Jazz was still largely an ensemble music, with improvisation being a matter of embellishment and embroidery rather than the streams of spontaneous melody that would characterize it later.

THE HOME OF NEW ORLEANS JAZZ

"New Orleans" Jazz found its new home in the black quarter of Chicago known as the South Side. By the 1920s Chicago's South Side had a population of about 100,000.

Young middleclass whites from all over America, drawn by the incredible vitality of this new music, began flocking to Chicago's South Side to hear the new music played by its acknowledged masters. The King Oliver band became so popular that Lincoln Gardens staged "midnight rambles" specifically for white fans.

THE CHIGACOANS

An early illustration of Jazz's universal appeal and adaptability were the guys loosely referred to as the "Chicagoans" (mainly guitarist **Eddie Condon**, clarinetists **Benny Goodman**, **Pee Wee**

Russell, **Frankie Teschemacher**, and **"Mezz" Mezrow**, drummer **Gene Krupa**, trumpeters **Mugsy Spanier** and **Jimmy McPhartland**, saxophonist **Bud Freeman**). The Chicagoans were well-educated college dropouts and intellectuals—well-trained white musicians who

took Jazz every bit as seriously as the New Orleans players—especially once they'd heard King Oliver and Louis Armstrong.

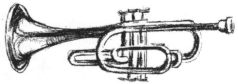

Along came Bix Beiderbecke, whose horn (according to Eddie Condon) "sounded like a girl saying yes."

Bix Beiderbecke, the cornettist from Davenport, Iowa, was the first white player considered a true Jazz giant by everybody. (*Almost* everybody. This is as good a place as any to admit that there is *nothing* in Jazz that *everyone* agrees on. In Jazz, everything is a split decision.)

Bix Beiderbecke picked a pack of pickled white guys, including guitarist Eddie Condon and clarinettist Pee Wee Russell, and they started a group. Bix not only knew how to play, he knew how to listen. Every chance he got, Bix went to study the moves of King Oliver, Louis Armstrong and other Black Einsteins of Jazz.

Bix Beiderbecke

The **"Chicago Style"** developed in the late 1920s. Big bands using written orchestrations appeared. Groups led by **Fletcher Henderson** (with scores by **Don Redman**), **Paul Whiteman** (with Bix Beiderbecke), **Chick Webb, Jimmie Lunceford,** and **Benny Moten** developed swing, characterized by a regular rhythm and the contrasting sounds of the sections of the band.

Fine musicians like the dazzling young Pittsburg pianist **Earl Hines** contributed the Chicago Jazz scene, but, even though Jazz was spreading faster than ever, Chicago's role in Jazz's history was coming to an end. By the end of the 20s, most of the major Chicago musicians, black and white, had moved to New York, the burgeoning center of America's entertainment business.

Earl "Fatha" Hines

The first commercial radio broadcasts took place in 1920; with in a couple years, there were over 500 stations.

And New York's Harlem had already become the capital of urban black America...

Harlem Renaissance

"The city's Harlem Renaissance began in the 1920s. Black poetry, art, music, literature, and philosophy flowered, partly encouraged by the optomism about the perfectability of the human spirit that had fueled the religious revivalism of the previous century."
-- From JAZZ—- by John Fordham

1920 - 30s
New York...

New York hadn't contributed much to the early art of Jazz—but the business of Jazz was another story. New York was a huckster's town: it sold things. It was the center of the entertainment industry, so it sold entertainment.

(You want a message, call Western Union.)

(You want Art? I'll give you one twice as big for half the price.)

New York owned the song publishing industry (Tin Pan Alley). New York was zeroing in on the emerging record industry. And most of the new radio stations. However ...

Despite all the cultural and commercial advantages of New York, the black South had given Jazz a spirit fire that the Show Biz City Slickers couldn't match and didn't quite know how to sell. The sharp end of New Orleans music was too fierce and raucous for a mass market and its overtly raunchy sound made the connection between dance and sex a little too obvious for some.

SAXOPHONE HOME

The music industry's problem—how to make Jazz tame enough for a mass market without smothering its vitality—had been solved on the West Coast around 1915. **Ferde Grofe**, a white arranger familiar with both European classical and gettin' down dance music, was experimenting with symphonic techniques for a dance band, using saxophones (seldom used outside of vaudeville) to carry a theme and contrasting it with written parts for other instruments.

KING OF JAZZBURGERS

Paul Whiteman, a bandleader with a background similar to Grofe's, slicked up his popular dance band with Grofe's classy arrangements. Whiteman's "symphonic jazz" was a great success (he sold three million copies of his first record in 1922) so humble Paul billed himself as the King of Jazz.

(Imagine the fat guy in Laurel & Hardy with slicked back hair and a skinny moustache—taking himself *verrry serrrriously*—and you have the spittin image of Paul Whiteman, King of Jazz!)

WhiteMan Speak with Melodious Forked Tongue

In 1924, the King of Jazz staged a concert in New York's Aeolian Hall to show the universe how far he had moved from "discordant early Jazz to the melodious from of the present." (Whiteman speak with forked tongue.) **George Gershwin** introduced his famous (arguably overrated) Rhapsody in Blue at the same melodious concert.

(Must've been a helluva night for Jazz lovers).

Fletcher Henderson: An Unheralded Giant

At about the same time that El Porko was Christening himself the King of Jazz, Fletcher Henderson was beginning to realize that a college degree in chemistry didn't help a young black man become a chemist. So, after a gig as a pianist for Black Swan, the first black record company, he became a bandleader.

At first his music sounded like Paul Whiteman's.

After awhile, he allowed bursts of real Jazz to take little bites out of the "melodious" choir of saxophones. Then he hired some real Jazz improvisers to add little bolts of lightning. Then he found ways of using the saxophones and brass sections in contrasting voicings.

In 1924, Fletcher Henderson brought Louis Armstrong, the godliest improviser in the 1920s universe, to join his New York band. Henderson and his chief arranger Don Redman had revolutionized big band Jazz so brilliantly, so thoroughly, and so convincingly that Paul Whitebread hired Bix Beiderbecke to spice up his blubbery band with some of Bix's vicious cornet solos.

HARLEM RENAISSANCE

The night is beautiful
So the faces of my people.

The stars are beautiful
So the eyes of my people.

Beautiful also is the sun
Beautiful also are the souls of my people.

-- Langston Hughes, "My People"

New York's **Harlem Renaissance** bgan in the 1920s. Black poetry, art, music, literature, and philosophy flowered. Harlem night spots attracted a huge white audience, who travelled through Harlem like it was East Berlin. **Duke Ellington's** band, first at the Kentucky Club, then the Cotton Club, thrived on a frequently caricatured image of African life. Ellington's famous "Black and Tan Fantasy" was composed to both celebrate and mock the "noble savage" that well-meaning white folks had replaced real black human beings with.

Harlem didn't just buzz in the night spots. Rent parties and parlor socials, where tenants hired musicians to play in their own homes and charged a small fee to cover the week's rent, created open houses for boogie-woogie pianists and technically masterful stride pianists like **Fats Waller** and **James P. Johnson** .

The music industry developed "race" labels specifically for black shops. The famous blues singer Bessie Smith spearheaded a blues boom that made a lot more money for recording companies like Columbia Records than it did for the singers.

Fate Waller

Bessie Smith

In 1929, the Stock Market crashed and so did the blues. During the Depression, America preferred to bury its head in the sand of Hollywood musicals. Nobody wanted anything as real as the blues.

Meanwhile, back at the Cotton Club ...

DUKE ELLINGTON

Duke reigned over the Cotton Club during its most celebrated period (1927 to 1931). By the early thirties, the Duke's bluesy version of symphonic Jazz had displaced Paul Whiteman in the popularity polls.

The Jazz Age died with the Great Depression.

But the Swing Age was about to be born.

Swing...
Swing...
Swing...

T hings were so bad during the Depression that prominent black musicians like Louis Armstrong, Duke Ellington, and Coleman Hawkins went to Europe to play. Sidney Bechet shined shoes to keep a friend's tailoring business from going under. "Territory bands" in shabby buses lived on the road and played for peanuts.

A BAND LIKE LOUIS

In 1934, the Fletcher Henderson band, which had done so much to make a big Jazz ensemble swing like Louis Armstrong, fell apart. Henderson had relied on his arranger, Don Redman, to expand the voicing for that elusive concept, swing. What Armstrong's trumpet did was to suggest rhythms spinning around rhythms, the beat of an improvised melody line whirling away from the core of an underlying rhythm but snapping back to it before it lost its center. Using a bigger band, divided into brass, reeds, and rhythm sections, Don Redman developed ensemble playing that sounded like an Armstrong solo and set the brass and reeds exchanging rousing harmonized riffs. This gave the whole outfit an energy that was intensified when the soloists played.

NECESSITY IS THE MUTHA

Redman and Henderson had this style working by 1931, but for the most part only the Harlem audiences knew it. Duke Ellington, Chick Webb, Earl Hines, had not been far behind. Henderson absorbed the method from Redman, who had derived it from a mixture of Armstrong's improvising and an understanding of the orchestral methods of Paul Whiteman and Ferde Grofe. Henderson improved on it himself once there were no sidekicks to call on.

Stompin' at the Savoy

The Depression had left Henderson, like everyone else, in financial trouble until a record company scout named John Hammond arranged for him up to provide charts for Benny Goodman, a young classically trained bandleader and clarinettist. Goodman was one of twelve children from an Eastern European Jewish family, whose prodigious talents were seen by has father as the family's ticket out of the ghetto.

Benny the kid was a fulltime pro by age 14. One of his models was a Detroit band that mixed New York suave with blunt midwestern blues, the Casa Loma Orchestra. Goodman and his manager both noticed that, despite the Depression, Casa Loma was a big hit on college campuses.

SINK OR SWING

In August 1935, Goodman's band, featuring trumpeter Bunny Berrigan and drummer Gene Krupa, played the Palomar Ballroom in Los Angeles. Goodman started out playing soft dance music to an audience of bored college students.

As a sink - or - swim gesture, he launched into Fletcher Henderson's arrangement of Jelly Roll Morton's "King Porter Stomp" -- New Orleans and Harlem united via the Jewish ghetto. The audience roared, the commercial breakthrough for a hot, vigorous, up-tempo, big band jazz in the black style had come, and Goodman was on the way to being dubbed the King of Swing."
-- From *JAZZ*—by John Fordham

The spread of radio and the end of the Depression helped the boom in Swing, as did Goodman's age, race, and talent. He was younger than all the Jazz pioneers, whose music seemed rooted in the Roaring Twenties. He looked like the boys in college campus audiences and he played with a mix of improvisational attack and European scrupulolusness that rang bells with a young educated audience all over the States.

Swing and dance were inseparable. At Harlem's Savoy Ballroom, lindy-hoppers developed the style to early swing, encouraging the transition to an even four-four beat to accompany a fluid, flowing dance idiom.

THE KING OF SWING

Five years after his California success, Goodman was an international star who brought Jazz even into the classical concert halls with the famous 1938 Carnegie Hall "Spirituals to Swing" show. He was also instrumental in bringing about mixed-race bands when he hired pianist Teddy Wilson, vibraharpist Lionel Hampton, and guitarist Charlie Christian.

THE DUKE OF HARLEM

Not only did white bandleaders like Glenn Miller, Bob Crosby, and the Dorsey brothers benefit from Goodman's success with this new wider audience, but many of these new converts to swing began to notice the fairly brilliant band(s) of Duke Ellington, who seemed to be constantly renewing both himself and his music, often by turning to a Jazz version of what classical composers call "impressionism" or "program music"—music that tries to evoke certain emotions, or to "describe"—musically—certain places and situations ...

"You hear fights, you smell dinner, you hear people making love. You hear the radio... You smell coffee... You hear people praying, fighting, snoring... I tried to put all that in Harlem Air Shaft."

-- Duke Ellington, talking about his piece, Harlem Air Shaft.

THE COUNT OF KANSAS CITY

In Kansas City, a simpler, bluesier music had been cooking since the 1920s, most notably in the Benny Moten outfit, featuring saxophonist Ben Webster and pianist William "Count" Basie. When Moten died (during a tonsillectomy operation!), Basie formed a band of his own, using Moten's ideas and many of his players. When the band came to New York, it became almost as popular as Benny Goodman's—and it changed Goodman's music.

It changed Jazz! Jo Jones, Basie's drummer, led the way toward a new approach to rhythm, with his looser, floating time and Basie himself pioneered a more restrained way of playing piano. Basie, like Ellington, seemed to cut through the different "schools" and appeal to nearly all Jazz players.

Coleman Hawkins (tenor saxophone), Art Tatum (piano), Roy Eldridge (trumpet), and Lester Young (tenor saxophone) were the individual stars of the day. Their style of solo improvisation grew in influence during this period, which also produced Billie Holiday, generally considered the greatest singer in the history of Jazz.

Meanwhile ...

Swing, for all its sound and fury, was a fairly rigid music, with fairly rigid rules. If there is one constant impulse that characterizes Jazz, it is the need to break the rules—even if they're your own. (*Especially* if they're your own.)

Swing couldn't last, everyone knew that. But not everyone was ready for the radical jazz movement that followed ...

Intermission

RACISM IN JAZZ

What Racism?

The Original Dixieland Jazz Band got the credit, money, and fame. Paul Whiteman was the King of Jazz, Benny Goodman was the King of Swing, Hollywood made nice movies about Bix Beiderbecke, Benny Goodman, Glenn Miller, the Dorsey brothers, Red Nichols, and other "Jazz greats!"

And when bands were finallyh integrated, Black musicians often couldn't eat in the same restaurants, sleep in the same hotels, or take a leak in the same urinals as their palefaced brothers -- but at least they were paid a lot less money than the wghite guys!

Racism? _What_ racism?

You'd have to be some kind of malcontent misfit to read racism into THAT!

BeBOP...
the '40s

Every art form has times when it courts its audience and times when it tells its audience to screw off. If Swing was Jazz that played down (or sucked up) to its audience, Bebop was Jazz that gave its audience The Finger.

The Finger (so to speak) was an earnest young man from Kansas City named **Charlie Parker.** In 1935, the Kansas City music scene was thriving -- the joints were open all night, pay was $1.25 a night, there were about 15 bands in town, plus Lester Young, Count Basie, Mary Lou Williams -- so Bird, a self-taught 15-year-old alto sax player, quit school to become a musician.

After a few legendary humiliations, he joined Jay McShann's bluesy swing band where he began playing with the harmonic potential in the chords of songs, and in the process, gaving more notes to juggle in his high-speed solos.

After a minute or two in Chicago, Bird went to New York, all the while searching for the way to play the music inside him: "I could hear it sometimes but I couldn't play it."

It was during this period that Bird experienced "an epiphany" after which he could *finally* play what he'd been hearing.

> <u>Technically</u>: by making a melody line of the higher intervals of a chord—and then using appropriate changes for that new chord-derived melody line—Bird could play "what i'd been hearing:" **bebop!**

Bird didn't invent Bebop, at least not by himself. **Art Tatum** and Coleman Hawkins had long been doing something similar. (So had modern European classical musicians.) People like Lester Young , Roy Eldridge, Count Basie, and Jo Jones were only a step away from playing it... but that last step was the hardest to take. It needed the reckless energy of guys with nothing to lose, like the young sidemen who met in the after-hours joints in New York.

Kenny Clarke

DIZ & KLOOK

One of the real pioneers of Bebop was drummer Kenny Clarke. Inspired by the work of Count Basie's Jo Jones, Clark wanted to create more tension in the music by setting contrasting rhythms against each other. He had acquired the nickname of 'Klook' in imitation of his drumming, which fiddled around the edges of the regular beat—unlike the steady thump of Swing.

Clark was with the Teddy Hill Swing band, which happened to include a free-spirited young trumpeter called **John Birks "Dizzy" Gillespie**, who was already experimenting with Swing harmony.

MINTON'S PLAYHOUSE

In 1940, Teddy Hill fired Klook for excessively weird playing, then rehired him a year later to put together a group for M i n t o n ' s Playhouse in Harlem. Clark sought out other gents who shared his far-out ideas and in no time at all he came up with Dizzy Gillespie and **Thelonious Monk**, an inventive pianist who used odd chords and left unexpected cliff-hanging spaces in his music.

Charlie Parker, Thelonious Monk and Dizzy Gillespie

Meanwhile, at another Harlem jamming joint called Monroe's Uptown House, Charlie Parker was surviving on a cut of the door money. Klook, dazzled by Parker, brought him to Minton's and together, Dizzy, Bird, Klook and Monk set about reinventing Jazz.

Eric Velasquez

No single one of them, including Parker, had seen clean to the end of Bebop. Each of them heard a fragment of the future, but it wasn't until they came together that "modern Jazz" was born.

CHANGES

It's hard to imagine, but after a full night of playing their regular "jobs" on the popular swing circuit, established stars like Coleman Hawkins, Duke Ellington, and Count Basie came to Minton's to let off some steam and get friendly with the radical new music.

Despite their good intentions, they didn't find it easy to fit in. To traditional jazz musicians—and to new audiences—Bebop sounded like the soloists entered too early or too late, left phrases hanging, or were playing out of rhythm and in the wrong key. In swing, the important notes in a phrase or the moment of a chord change coincided with the traditional strong beat. Bebop reversed these musical signposts to hit weak, offbeats instead.

THE ONE AND ONLY

Other musicians played crucial roles in Bebop's development, but Charlie Parker was its uncontested genius. Parker's sense of time and location within the structure of a tune was so solid that he could abandon the framework for long improvised stretches, skydiving into distant keys, but always landing on his feet. Bebop's horn players were further encouraged to take risks by adventurous drummers like Kenny Clark and **Max Roach.**

REVOLUTIONARY CLASSICS

Swing bandleaders like pianist Earl Hines, singer-trumpeter Billy Eckstine, and Woody Herman, encouraged the bebop players. Coleman Hawkins, who played with nearly the same harmonic sense as the new dudes, encouraged the boppers to record.

The recordings from that first wave of Bebop are now jazz classics. A band that included Charlie Parker and Max Roach played New York's Three Deuces in 1944, and a Coleman Hawkins-led band with Dizzy Gillespie made the first Bop recordings.

In 1945 Diz and Bird began the sensational succession of small-group recordings that produced "Groovin' High," "Billie's Bounce," "Now's the Time," and "Ko-Ko."

The second of Norman Granz's Jazz at the Philharmonic concerts (January, 1946) featured some of the greatest Jazz musicians in the world, including Charlie Parker.

Let's pause for a second and talk about the music:

What exactly was *Bebop*?

The Music...
Although it seemed like a radical break with the past, Bebop was more evolution than revolution.

Although its rhythmic accents were more unpredictable, Bop still basically used Swing's fast four-four beat.

And although Bop involved improvisation over chords (instead of melodies), the chords were just modified versions of the old chords.

(i.e., Blues and Pop songs.)

Bebop made Jazz at once both...

more European...
"...as Bach might have sounded if he had been acquainted with the blues and African time."

and more African...
"...the style of its drumming went closer to recapturing the mysterious, talkative polycurrents" of African music.
-- from *JAZZ* by John Fordham

Some smart people say that Africa had no "Art" music. (Art is extra—beautiful but useless—whereas, in Africa, they say, all music was part of some social function.

That may be true about Africa but it's not true about Jazz.

Bebop was Jazz's **Art Music.**

FUSION

At the end of the 1940s, Dizzy Gillespie, the most show-biz of the beboppers, formed a band that fused Latin-American dance music with jazz, further uniting Jazz with its rhythmic ancestry.

"The people of the calypso, the rhumba, the samba and the rhythms of Haiti all have something in common from the mother of their music. Rhythm. The basic rhythm, because Mama Rhythm is Africa."
-- from *"To Be or Not to Bop"* by Dizzy Gillespie

Diz brought in guys like Chano Pozo, the Cuban percussionist who helped reintroduce Jazz to its polyrhythmic West African roots (before Mr. Pozo was iced).

Q: What is the silliest name you can thing of for the fusion of Bebop and Cuban music?

A: *CuBop.*

INSPIRATION

Dizzy Gillespie's two-month tour of European concert halls in 1948—plus the Paris Jazz Festival of 1949, featuring Charlie Parker and Miles Davis, showed Americans that a sophisticated audience for the new music existed outside the States.

The inspiration of Parker and Gillespie encouraged many brilliant young musicians to follow in their wake, including Fats Navarro and Clifford Brown (trumpets), and Dexter Gordon, Sonny Rollins, and Sonny Stitt (saxophones).

But that wasn't all they encouraged. Bebop was not only a music, it was a lifestyle...

THE HIPSTER

Various theories, all of them good, none of them convincing, take turns trying to explain the interesting critter called the Hipster that appeared in the 1940s.

The Hipster had two distinctly different styles, exquisitely embodied by Charlie Parker and Dizzy Gillespie.

DIZ & BIRD

Dizzy Gillespie invented the Hipster *look*: beret, sunglasses, goatee—think of it as the greatgrandaddy of the Beatnik look.

Bunk Johnson

Diz was also a funny, ballbustin', cheerful man. His brilliant music was an outgrowth of his brilliant restless wit. Diz enjoyed the hell out of life. He seemed to enjoy his own playing in the way that Pavarotti enjoys his own voice—as if to say, 'Holy shit, that's amazing!' Diz was the Hipster as ecstacy-driven-oddball.

Parker was the opposite -- the Doomed Hipster. The Jazzman - as - victim. (See Parker's bio in PART TWO for more on Bird's life -- no need to depress you now.)

BACKLASH

There were two fascinating counter reactions to bop:

Bebop's zigzag melodies, breathless tempos, and calculus-like complexity led to a revival of listener-friendly New Orleans jazz. (One of the highlights was the <u>un</u>retirement of the legendary cornetist **Bunk Johnson**.)

Bop's backlash also led to a music that used many of the innovations of bebop, but caressed the audience with a softer sound instead of shaking it until its teeth rattled.

The **Gerry Mulligan/Chet Baker** band became the sound that most people identified with Cool Jazz.

Mulligan, with trumpeter Chet Baker, performed a quietly conversational kind of Bebop without a piano, which became commercially very successful, not the least because Baker—who resembled James Dean and played deadpan, romantic trumpet...was a popular crooner, too.
-- from JAZZ by John Fordham

The 50s – Birth [& death] of the Cool

In the late 1940s, young musicians from L.A. to Leningrad wanted to sound like Charlie Parker. The best of the young Jazzmen were so intent on testing and developing their own voices that they started functioning more as soloists that other musicians played *for* instead of *with*.

Everybody wanted to be a genius.
It was only a matter of time until a counter-revolution set in.

BIRTH OF THE COOL
In 1948, trumpeter Miles Davis assembled a nine-piece band for a few gigs in New York. The "nonet" played a three-week engagement at the Royal Roost, at Broadway and 47th Street. Miles insisted that a sign be put in front of the club reading, "Arrangements by Gerry Mulligan, Gil Evans, and John Lewis."

The following year, the group cut a record. The music wasn't explosive and bluesy like Parker's Bop. It was an ethereal, drifting music that used French horns, complex arrangements, and delicately woven solos. The tracks that this new band cut in 1949 and 1950 became known as the *Birth of the Cool*.

INVENTING MILES
According to Jazz apocrypha, Miles had taken stock of his own limitations as a trumpeter and decided that trying to play faster, higher, and hotter than everyone else was a doomed enterprise. (Who could play faster, higher, and hotter than Dizzy?) On first hearing, you can't help but be astonished by what fast players Bird and Diz were. After a few hearings, you realize that, not only were they fast players, they were impossibly fast thinkers—especially Bird.

Miles, unlike Bird and Diz, wasn't a blazingly fast thinker.

But he was a deep thinker.

So Miles took the opposite approach: he would play lower, slower and cooler than anybody else. Like Bird, but for different reasons, Miles believed that improvisation based on pop songs limited Jazz by confining it to short, song-length forms.

MILES AND GIL

Miles brought in Gil Evans, a young Canadian who had studied the works of European classical composers like Debussy and the works of Harlem classical composers like Duke Ellington, and who had been the key arranger in Claude Thornhill's underrated orchestra. (Other big bands, most notably Stan Kenton's, also leaned toward a Europeanized Jazz with longer, suitelike pieces and devices as likely to be drawn from Debussy as from Charlie Parker.)

MULLIGAN & KONITZ

Miles also wanted soloists more like himself, guys who didn't play as if they'd heard someone firing a starting pistol. He found two white saxophones, baritone Gerry Mulligan and alto Lee Konitz, both from the Thornhill band. Konitz had clearly been influenced by Parker—who hadn't?—but under the guidance of the tough-minded blind Chicago pianist Lennie Tristano, he used Bird's ideas in his own way. Mulligan's sound was influenced by the only other saxophonist whose influence on horn players still rivaled Parker's—the poetic, rhapsodic Lester Young.

LENNY TRISTANO

By the time "Cool" Jazz arrived in the early 50s, Lester Young was sickly and erratic, while a whole flock of successful young "Cool" saxophonists—Konitz, Mulligan, Art Pepper, Wayne Marsh, Paul Desmond, Stan Getz—damn near cloned his sound.

The true giants of The Cool, however, were Lenny Tristano and Miles, who had nothing in common except their refusal to let

Jazz improvisation be limited by pop song chords and solos that raced like high speed car chases.

Tristano was a purist who hated flashy effects and crowd-pleasing cliches. If young Jazz players tried to emulate Parker's sax, Tristano's disciples played like pianists (even if they were sax players) spinning long lines of melody without raising their voices. Drummers were just timekeepers—none of the polyrhythmic gear-shifting of Max Roach or Kenny Clark.

Tristano's music was too cerebral for some, but in liberating Jazz from popular song forms, he opened the door for the free Jazz movement that would come later.

WEST COAST JAZZ

Although the Cool sound is identified with West Coast Jazz, much of the music from the West wasn't Cool at all, even when it revealed a scholarly interest in formal musical experiements.

The Dave Brubeck gang, one of the most popular Jazz groups of the early 60s, experimented with European classical forms and time signatures that were complex even by Jazz standards. Brubeck's playing style was anything but Cool: he beat the hell out of his piano and his drummer Joe Morello was as polyrhythmically perverse as any hot Jazz drummer. Sax man Paul Desmond, on the other hand, was as Cool as it gets.

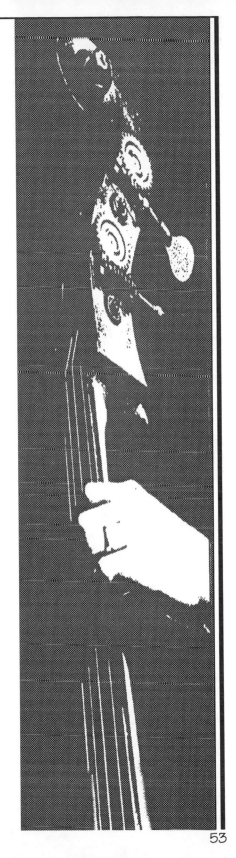

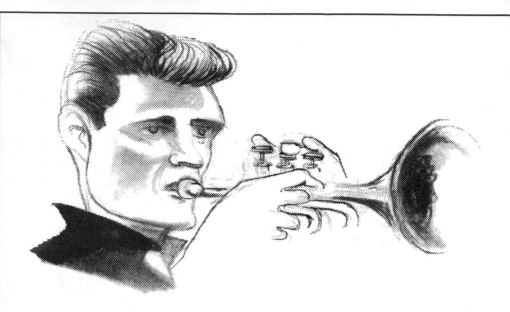

GERRY & CHET

Gerry Mulligan and Chet Baker played a kind of quiet Bop that made large money largely because Chet Baker looked like a stoned James Dean, played romantic trumpet like a spayed Miles Davis, and sang romantic ballads with Buddhalike detachment.

THE MJQ

The Cool sound's most durable East Coast group was the popular Modern Jazz Quartet, which combined European baroque music (classically trained pianist John Lewis liked rondos and Bach-like fugues) and blues from marvellous Bop vibraphonist Milt Jackson.

HOT WEST COAST JAZZ

Some of the West Coast players were extremely uncool. There were white guys with fire in their eyes like altoist Art Pepper and black guys like Frank Morgan who, on a good day, could sound almost as passionate as Bird. Flugelhorn player Shorty Rogers led bands that played robust, boppish music and a group led by pianist Hampton Hawes, with saxophonist Harold Land played Bebop as fierce as any on 52nd Street. Dexter Gordon, one of the bluesiest players in Jazz, is also from California.

HOWEVER...

The Minister of Cool was still Miles Davis. Although he had been in the forefront of the creation of the Cool, he was also in the thick of the reaction that murdered it: hard Bop. Miles, however, would have his personal problems ... .

... late one night in the spring of 1953, Miles was standing outside Birdland looking every bit the junkie when he was approached by Max Roach. Max took a good look at Miles and slapped two crisp $100 bills in his hand and told him that he was "looking good."

Max, who had been like a brother to Miles since the early Bird days, was clean and taking care of himself, and his gesture so humiliated Miles that Miles called his father and returned to St. Louis to get clean.
-- from MILES DAVIS FOR BEGINNERS by Daryl Long

Unfortunately, Miles' first attempt wasn't successful.

HARD BOP—THE DEATH OF THE COOL

At first Cool Jazz was seen as elegant and lyrical. By the mid-1950s, it began to feel repressed, emotionally empty, and uptight. That was partly due to rock and roll—especially Elvis, a Memphis white boy who had the rhythmic drive and fire in his trousers that had once been the domain of Jazz.

THE UNCOOL SCHOOL

Although the Cool school had hogged the spotlight (and the cash flow) for a few years, the overheated boppers had continued to flourish, especially in the black neighborhoods of Northeastern cities. Bass virtuoso Charles Mingus and drummer Max Roach had set up

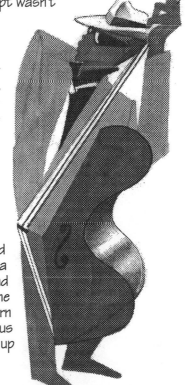

their own record company to specialize in new Jazz. In the mid-1950s, Mingus formed a workshop to explore Bebop, Gospel, and Blues—and to create compositions and arrangements large and various enough to include them all. Powerhouse tenor sax improviser Sonny Rollins worked first with Miles and Monk, then with Max Roach and Dizzy's young protege Clifford Brown.

Dexter Gordon formed an exciting two-tenor part-nership with Wardell Gray.

Drummer
Art Blakey formed the **Jazz Messengers**, a group that introduced some of the best young talent in Jazz until Blakey's death in 1990.

THE VOID

In 1955, at the age of 34, Charlie Parker died. He left behind some great music, some heroin addicts, a line of graffiti ("Bird died for our sins") that appeared on outhouse walls all over America...and an enormous void.

Charlie Parker was a hard act to follow. In the beginning, his monumental influence had been liberating—it seemed to open up infinite possibilities for Jazz—but ultimately, Bird's genius was so overwhelming that it left no room for future players.

Like the great experimental novelist James Joyce, Bird had pretty much burned down the field he'd liberated.

There had to be another way.
There was...but it was still addicted to heroin.

"I was a good friend of Ray Robinson. Watching him train as diligently as he did, it made me break my heroin habit. The man was in shape ten months out of the year. Goddamn! And then the beauty, how he did things, I never saw anybody like that."

-- from "Miles Davis Is A Living Legend and You're Not" by Mark Rowland -- *MUSICIAN* Magazine

MILESTONES 1955
- Miles tears up the Newport Jazz Festival by playing ... Monk's "Round Midnight" with a mute.
- Miles ties Dizzy for DownBeat kudos.
- Miles puts together ... the combo that would make him a legend, featuring ... John Coltrane

"The music that we were playing ... was so bad that it used to send chills through me at night." -- Miles

-- from *MILES DAVIS FOR BEGINNERS* by Daryl Long

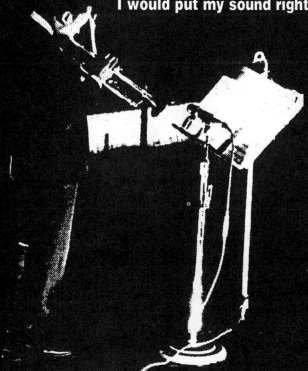

"Trane would play some weird, great shit, and Cannonball would take it in the other direction, and I would put my sound right down the middle or float over it ... might play real fast, or Buzzzzz .... This would take Trane someplace else .... and then Paul's anchoring all this creative tension between the horns, and Red's laying down his light, hip shit, and Philly Joe pushing everything ... Man, that was too hip and bad."

-- from *MILES: the AUTOBIOGRAPHY* with Quincy Troupe

Miles' new group's first recording was **Milestones**:

The 1960s : Modal Jazz

(Miles sings flamenco)

Milestones quietly featured an innovation that would free Jazz from the constraints of Bebop: **Modal improvisation**. But it was the group's next album that would redefine Jazz.

KIND OF BLUE

In 1959, Miles Davis astonished, reinvigorated, and simplified Jazz with the haunting, trancelike, *Kind of Blue*, the most influential Jazz recording since the mid-40s. It featured one of the finest Jazz combos ever: Cannonball Adderly on alto sax, Bill Evans/Winton Kelly on piano, Paul Chambers on bass, Jimmy Cobb on drums, and John Coltrane—blessed, obsessed, driven—on tenor sax.

Coltrane was Miles' diametric opposite. Where Miles' playing was spare and full of elegant zen silences, Coltrane played the tenor like it was a machinegun. (In his hands, it was.)

> ## *Kind of Blue* was the first big recording of "Modal" Jazz.

MODAL JAZZ

Jazz had backed itself into a corner. Bebop was a bold, brilliant music, but it was so complex—with harmonic "rules" as strict and formal as Baroque—that you had to be a mathematical genius to *think* it and a technical wizard to *play* it. Jazz players began to feel hemmed in. Modal Jazz arose in reaction to the complexity—and the limitations—of Jazz based on chords.

> Complexity: Jazz lore has it that John Coltrane's solos in his album *Giant Steps* ran at around 100 chord changes per minute!

> Limitations: Miles: "When you're based on chords, you know at the end of 32 bars that the chords run out and there's nothing to do but repeat what you've just done—with variations."

In a search for a simpler, more atmospheric framework, Modal Jazz was based on a single scale or sequence of scales. It is closer to Indian music, because it works on horizontal patterns rather than vertical ones like chords. Composer/bandleader George Russell, one of Jazz's great theoreticians, goosed the process along with his *The Lydian Chromatic Concept of Tonal Organization*. John Coltrane studied Modal structure from both early European and Eastern music.

MILES, THE SINGER

Miles, who never stayed in one place for long, veered away from the approach he pioneered in *Kind of Blue* and cut another record with Gil Evans' orchestra. (Miles and Gil had recorded *Miles Ahead* and *Porgy and Bess*.) Gil often referred to Miles as a "singer." Miles sang through his trumpet. If you doubt it, listen to Miles on songs like "Stella by Starlight" or "I Love You Porgy."

Let us admit that a few uptight Jazz critics—guys who treat Jazz like a temple you have to guard against invaders—consider the Miles Davis/Gil Evans collaborations mere elevator music.

Even so, *Sketches of Spain* was so different that many of the most tightass critics liked it. On the longest cut, "Concerto de Aranjuez for Guitar and Orchestra," Gil Evans supplied the orchestra, and Miles was, well, sort of ... a guitar! In the remaining pieces, Miles does *not* play his version of a "Spanishy" trumpet—he is, more than ever, Miles the *singer*. But this time, Miles is a Spanish flamenco singer. If you have never heard a Spanish flamenco singer, do yourself a favor: listen to one alongside *Sketches of Spain*. Damn, but Miles could sing.

Describing a cut from *Sketches*, critic Martin Williams wrote:

> **"...[Gil] Evans provided fanfares for a Saeta, a traditional Holy Week vocal lament for the dead Christ, and Miles Davis plays it with a stark, deeply felt communal anguish that Jazz has not heard since King Oliver."**

Miles plays it with a stark, deeply felt communal anguish... .

Remember those words: not only are they true and beautiful (thank you, Mr. Williams), but we'll need them again later.

His Favorite Things

Like Miles, John Coltrane also bopped away from the Modal implications of *Kind of Blue* on his next album, *Giant Steps*. Even so, Trane's playing, which included impossible-seeming "split notes," where Coltrane played several notes (or *tones*) at the same time, seemed to fly at you with such simultaneous fury that they became known as "sheets of sound."

In 1960, shortly after *Giant Steps*, Trane discovered the soprano sax, Modal improvising, and the song "My Favorite Things."

That's when all hell broke loose. John Coltrane became—hard as it was to believe—famous.

Critic Martin Williams expressed the disbelief that many felt:

"It was almost impossible for a man to be as much of a technician, artist, and explorer as Coltrane and still have the kind of popular following he had. What did he tell that audience? In what new and meaningful things did his music instruct them?"

We'll have a go at answering that question later. For now, try this on for size:

A psychiatrist trying to explain the soul-force of John Coltrane: "It sounds like a man strapped down and finally screaming to be free."

-- from **JAZZ IS** by Nat Hentoff

SCREAMING TO BE FREE

Freedom, as every man with a lick of sense knows, is a bitch to achieve. In music, as in life, it doesn't happen overnight. It takes time and patience. For years, wise and patient Jazz players had been loosening Jazz's shackles, one by one, goosing Jazz along, inch by inch, toward ever-increasing, teensy-weensy bits of freedom.

Then one day—late 50s, early 60s—a guy comes along who doesn't know how difficult it is ... so he just TAKES it!

FREE JAZZ

While Miles and Coltrane and Mingus and Monk and other wise men were, each in their own way, inching toward freedom, a young rhythm and Blues brother from Texas decided, plain and simple, that his saxophone was free to do whatver in the hell it wanted.

     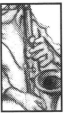 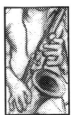

That was Ornette (squeak, squak, honk, hoot) Coleman.

He set Jazz free. He didn't like chords, so he *trashed* them!

("You can't do that!" "What do you mean, I *can't*? I just *did*!")

Ornette didn't like pianos, so he didn't use one.

Ornette's first New York gig was at the Five Spot in 1959.

Jazz trumpet legend Roy Eldridge had his own opinion of Ornette: "He's jiving, baby. He's putting everybody on."

Cecil's Beleagured Piano
Ornette's recordings *Something Else* and *Tomorrow Is the Question* ignited the Free Jazz movement ... and irritated the hell out of many Jazz lovers.

Please note:

Nobody loves jazz. People love Miles or Diexieland or Bop or Ellington or Swing or Free Jazz or Fusion or two, three or four of the above – but nobody loves jazz. It's too varied.

Ornette made the breakthrough, but players like pianist **Cecil Taylor** had been working along similar lines for years.

Correction: Nobody was "similar" to Cecil, who played his piano like a cross between Chopin and Mike Tyson. Drummer Jo Jones got so irritated that he threw a cymbal at Cecil. Miles, who took nobody's word for anything, went to Birdland to scope out Cecil firsthand. Miles, cursing and grumbling, walked out as Cecil continued banging avant gardely on his piano.

MEANWHILE ...

America was being asked to live up to its advertising and honor its promise of equality. In the late 50s, American soldiers began escorting black students into segregated southern schools.

In 1963, a month after Martin Luther King gave his "I have a dream" speech, four young black girls were killed in a church bombing in Alabama. America had a long way to go.

Archie Shepp, writer/musician/political activist, was one of the first to use his music—free and passionate Jazz—to support the struggle of black Americans. Others followed. Drummer **Max Roach** made *We Insist—Freedom Now Suite*. **Coleman Hawkins** & **Sonny Rollins** joined energies for *The Freedom Suite*.

Other black Americans joined energies with dead and live Europeans: **Cecil Taylor** and player/composer **Anthony Braxton** laced their Jazz with modern European classics.

Come to think of it, bassist/composer **Charles Mingus** had been doing that for years. (Mingus, never shy, mentioned that Jazz was finally catching up with him.)

British guitarist **John MacLaughlin**, influenced by both Jazz and Indian sitar music, played with great speed and beauty.,

British saxophonists **John Surman** and **Evan Parker** used Coltrane's music to inspire truly creative work of their own, as did Norwegian **Jan Garbarek** and dozens of others all over the world.

Hard core avant gardists like **Cecil Taylor, Ornette Coleman**, and Ornette's trumpeter **Don Cherry** usually felt more welcome in Europe than in America.

"Liberated" Jazz

Meanwhile, people who didn't love the music that Ornette or Cecil played, loved the music they *caused*:

By the mid-60s, **John Coltrane** moved in and out of Free Jazz. His new quartet (not quite Free, but *extremely* liberated)—**McCoy Tyner** (piano), **Jimmy Garrison** (bass), **Elvin Jones** (drums)—was so powerful that players *still* go to school on it.

Coltrane's major records of 1965, *Ascension, Meditation,* and *Kulu Se Mama,* featured the free-blowing **Archie Shepp** and the apocalyptic saxophone orgasms of Pharoah Sanders. Trane, as you may suspect from titles like *Ascension* and *Meditation,* was becoming increasingly spiritual. However ...

Sitar saint Ravi Shankar, who knew Coltrane well, said:

> **"I was much disturbed by his music. Here was a creative person who had become a vegetarian, who was studying yoga and reading the Bhagavad-Gita, yet in whose music I still hear much turmoil. I could not understand it."** (Maybe later.)

MEANWHILE, Miles Davis, who thought he hated Free Jazz, had put together one of the fiercest "liberated" groups ever: **Wayne Shorter** on sax, **Herbie Hancock** on keyboards, **Ron Carter** on bass, and spectacular **Tony Williams** on drums. (The group wasn't allowed to play in some clubs because Tony, a teenager, was too young to be in the bar.)

The group, in the right-on words of author John Fordham, "produced some of the most loose and explicitly emotional, yet emphatically shapely music he [Miles] had ever recorded." Amen.

MEANWHILE, people you never heard of were blowing up a storm.

One of them, **Sun Ra**, swore he was born on the planet Saturn.

Another, **Eric Dolphy,** played with brilliance on flute and alto sax, and with something approaching genius on the bass clarinet.

Some Jazzheads think Dolphy was better than Coltrane.

(I say, Why choose between two good things when you can have both?)

In a way, that was the spirit behind the Jazz of the 70s...

The 1970s: Fusion (and ConFusion)

By the late 60s, Bebop was museum music, Cool Jazz had bossa nova-ed itself into dentist's offices all over the world, Coltrane had died, and Free Jazz had died with him.

At roughly the same time, young people all over the world—millions of them—were unified by a new religion that seemed to be taking over the entire universe: Rock Music.

Jazz was rapidly losing its audience. Worse, to the young Rockers, Jazz (which was once so dangerous that you had to protect your daughters from its sinful influence) was as dated, dried up, irrelevant and useless as Pat Boone's shoes. Jazz was dying. But it was nothing personal. These were brand new people who looked at the world with new eyes and saw it for what it was:

THEY SAW

...teenage boys with testosterone for brains being rushed off to die for nothing in Vietnam before their hormones quieted down enough to realize that maybe <u>you</u> should *decide* what you're going to die for instead of letting the D.C. bullshit factory decide for you.

THEY SAW

...human beings being allowed to ride in the front of a bus—<u>allowed!</u>—*100 years after the Emancipation!* After *100 years of freedom*, you have to kiss some redneck's boot to eat in a lousy restaurant! And for that, they expect you to be grateful!

It was easy to see why those fresh-eyed young heroes decided that their parents had made a mess of the world. It wasn't hard to understand why they decided to throw out *everything* from that ugly, repressive, fake old world. Even if a few of the old things—like Jazz—*were* honest and real, they didn't have the time (or the wisdom) to make distinctions.

The unifying force of the new youth culture was Rock Music. *Their* music. *Created by* them. *Performed by* them.

Jazz was dying.

How do you know if jazz is dying?

*You check **Miles Davis'** record sales.*

Gotta be a smart ass, don't you?

*I'm not being a smart ass. **Miles** was -- by a mile -- the best selling Jazz artist in those days. If his record sales were going down -- and they were -- pity the other players*

Wrong: Jazz was dead

HOWEVER...

Despite the fact that Jazz was dead, **Miles Davis** and his band of brilliant young explorers (**Herbie Hancock, Wayne Shorter, Tony Williams, Ron Carter**) were birthing some of the most miraculous Jazz recordings ever, testing the limits, trying to balance freedom and structure. Trying to answer the question, *musically,* "How freely can we improvise without losing the music, before "the center doesn't hold?" How far can we go before we get lost?"

Herbie Hancock, the protean young pianist, said, "Sometimes we got lost out there. I mean *really lost.* But any time you got lost, Miles always knew it. He'd come in and play a few notes and bring it all back to the center."

THE PRINCE OF FUSION

Even as Miles and his crew were making brilliant music at the outer limits of Jazz, Miles had decided that Jazz was losing its natural audience—young black people—so he began listening to Sly and the Family Stone and Jimi Hendrix.

Slowly at first, Miles added new players—Chick Corea and Joe Zawinul on keyboards (mostly electric), British electric guitarist John McLaughlin, bassist Dave Holland and, eventually Jack DeJohnette on drums—and a lot of electricity.

He warmed up with *Filles de Kilimanjaro* and *In a Silent Way*, then in 1969 Miles did *Bitches Brew* and all hell broke loose.

"Bitches Brew is one of the most divisive jazz albums ever made. To some it is another of Miles' great steps forward, a session to put beside Birth of the Cool and Kind of Blue. To others it marked the point where he ceased to be of serious musical interest..."

-- from Jazz, The Essential CD Guide by Martin Gayford.

That, my darlins', was Fusion — the love-it or hate-it bastard child of **Jazz** and ROCK.

Jazz purists hated it. They didn't say it was lousy Jazz, they said it wasn't Jazz, *period!*

(The greatest insult a Jazz snob can drop on you is *not* to say you play lousy Jazz, it's to say, "That shit's *not Jazz.*")

Jazz-Rock Fusion brought people, ideas and money to Jazz. It also brought the soprano sax to Wayne Shorter.

SON OF MY FAVORITE THINGS

Ever since John Coltrane's blockbuster recording of "My Favorite Things," Professor Coltrane *owned* the soprano sax in Jazz.

Wayne Shorter (out of respect for the master?) waited until well after Coltrane's death before he took up the soprano sax. Jazz purists can get as persnickety as wine-tasters over some of the music on *Bitches Brew,* but Wayne Shorter's soprano sax solos are pure badass Jazz solos.

Nothing lasts forever. In 1976, Miles Davis, at one of the peaks of his career, dropped out. His explanation?

"I stopped hearing the music."

Robin, Tonto, Watson, and the Vandellas
Miles' sidekicks, now famous but without their Center, formed Fusion groups of their own.

Wayne Shorter and **Joe Zawinul** created **Weather Report**

Chick Corea (piano) started **Return to Forever**

Jack DeJohnette, Special Edition

Tony Williams, Lifetime

John MacLaughlin formed **The Mahavishnu Orchestra**

COMBINATAIONS & PERMUTATIONS

Although *Fusion* usually referred to the combination of Jazz & rock, the most interesting Fusions were generally *not* Jazz/Rock:

Chick Corea's Return to Forever fused Jazz and <u>Latin music</u> (which Diz had done in the 40s).

John McLaughlin's Mahavishnu Orchestra fused Free Jazz with <u>Indian sitar music</u>.

Although you can't quite call it Jazz, you can probably credit Jazz for the Fusion of Ravi Shankar's Indian <u>sitar</u> music with <u>classical violinist</u> Yehudi Menuin. And the Fusion of Shankar's <u>sitar</u> with the Japanese Koto Ensemble. (You really have to hear that one!)

(Speaking of Shankar: Do yourself a favor and listen to Uncle Ravi, *period!* Talk about "sheets of sound!" Shankar's sitar comes at you like 15 foot wave.)

Brazilian saxophonist Gato Barbieri, fused Free Jazz and <u>Brazilian</u>...orgasms?

South African pianist Abdullah Ibrahim fused indigenous African music with Jazz.

Artist	Instrument	Fused with...
Chick Corea	keyboards	Latin music
John MacLaughlin	free jazz guitar	Indian sitar
Ravi Shankar	Indian sitar	classical violin
Ravi Shankar	Indian sitar	Japanese Koto Ensemble
Gato Barbieri	free jazz saxophone	Brazilian music
Abdullah Ibrahim	keyboards	African music

DEFusion

It seems a trifle weird to refer to what Keith Jarrett does as "Fusion"—more like DEFusion, since he threw out everything but his piano. No sax, bass or drums. No electricity.

Just Keith and his acoustic piano. They call it Fusion because Keith, they say, fuses Jazz with classical. In reality, Keith, by fusing everything with everything, shows us that music is music.

Keith Jarrett's mid-70s **Köln Concert** is the best selling solo piano recording of all time. It deserves to be. If you're not careful, it can drive you into one or two fits of ecstacy.

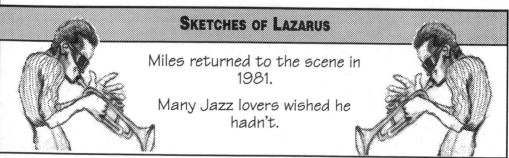

SKETCHES OF LAZARUS

Miles returned to the scene in 1981.

Many Jazz lovers wished he hadn't.

Counterpoint

Two or more melodies (each strong enough to stand alone) played simultaneously to produce a single musical fabric.

Women in Jazz and Jazz Singers

WOMEN IN JAZZ

Women have never been excluded from Jazz, but they've never been included either. Jazz, sad to say, has been approximately as sexist as the society from which it emerged. There have been a handful of female instrumentalists—almost all pianists—but they have been drastically underrepresented.

One of the earliest was **Lilian Hardin Armstrong** (1903-71). Lil studied for a concert career at Fisk University, but while still in her teens, she joined Freddie Keppard's Chicago band. She moved to King Oliver's band in 1920, where she met and married Louis Armstrong in 1924. (In case you're tempted to think that Lil's only claim to fame was being Louis' wife, note that she was playing with the best Jazz bands in the world for four years *before* she met Louis.) Lil played on many of Louis' famous "Hot Five" records; in 1925 she and Louis led their own band.

After she and Louis divorced (1932), Lil Armstrong led various all-star bands on a series of Decca recordings. In the early 50s, she split to Europe (primarily England and France), where she alternated between working as a solo pianist and playing with other expatriate Americans (like Sidney Bechet).

Two musicians who were/are so good that they almost always turn up on the most studly lists of Jazz instrumentalists are pianist Mary Lou Williams and composer/pianist Carla Bley.

Mary Lou Williams (1910-1981), a Bluesy pianist/arranger from Atlanta, was making records by age 17. Most of her early work was done in the Southwest with Andy Kirk's orchestra.

After several succesful years in Kansas City, Ms. Williams headed East and worked with Benny Goodman, Earl Hines, and Tommy Dorsey. In the 50s, she was an arranger for Ellington and became friendly with Bud Powell, Thelonious Monk, and Bebop.

Mary Lou Williams was described by critic Nat Shapiro as "the best example of a musician who has refused to be imprisoned by either style or tradition." She toured extensively in the 60s and 70s and taught at Duke University in North Carolina.

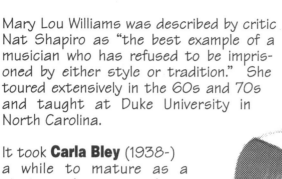

It took **Carla Bley** (1938-) a while to mature as a pianist and composer. In 1959 she married free Jazz pianist **Paul Bley** and became involved in the Jazz Composers Guild, a group that tried to buck the music establishment. Carla divorced Paul, married trumpeter **Mike Mantler**, and co-founded the Jazz Composer's Orchestra Association. In 1965 she toured Europe with sax player **Steve Lacy** in the Jazz Realities Quintet.

by Susan David

As a pianist, she was quirky, teasing with nice, easy melodies, then pulling the carpet out with dissonances and out-of-whack rhythms. Bley's greatest impact was as a composer. She hit her stride with *Escalator Over the Hill* (1968-71), a long, opera-like piece for a big band that took her three years to write.

by Susan David

(The recorded version features strong performances by **John McLaughlin, Don Cherry, Jack Bruce, Gato Barbieri**, and singer **Linda Ronstadt**.) Ms. Bley is still going strong.

Jazz may be America's only original art form, but Americans don't own it.

Toshiko Akiyoshi, born in Manchuria in 1929, chose Duke Ellington as her role model and for forty years, she has been one of Japan's finest Jazz artists. Ms. Akiyoshi studied classical music until she heard pianist **Teddy Wilson**.

She was so dazzled by Mr. Wilson's improvisation that she switched to Jazz. In 1947 she joined the Tokyo Jive Combo. In 1951 she formed her own group. The great Jazz pianist **Oscar Peterson** (visiting Japan with Norman Granz' Jazz at the Philharmonic) heard Akiyoshi and was so impressed that he persuaded Granz to record her. After being named Japan's leading Jazz pianist, the amazingly unegotistical Ms. Akiyoshi went to America to study Jazz at Boston's Berklee College of Music (1956-59).

For years Akiyoshi played like a lyrical Bud Powell (*lyrical, not feminine*; her playing is fierce) but she isn't easy to classify, partly because she has become an outstanding bandleader and composer. In 1972 she moved to Los Angeles with her husband **Lew Tabackin** and formed a big band, devoted mainly to playing her own compositions.

by Ron David

The band was so good that Lyons and Perlo (*Jazz Portraits*) called it "the most creative big band in Jazz"—but their records never sold well. (The reason? Simple but disgusting: RCA simply had no interest in promoting new Jazz!)

Jutta Hipp, a pianist born in Leipzig, Germany in 1929, started out playing like Lenny Tristano, the blind professor of cool, and ended up playing like Horace Silver, the father of Funk!

British-born pianist **Marian McPartland** started out with her husband, trumpeter **Jimmy McPartland**'s group, but made her mark with her own trio, playing in places like the Hickory House (NYC), one of Duke Ellington's hangouts.

Yeah well, Japan, Germany, England and all those other postcard places are nice but God lives in places like Detroit, LA and Philly...

Terry Pollard, a pianist and vibes player from Detroit who won the 1956 *Down Beat* critics' poll as the outstanding new vibes player, had her "fifteen minutes of success" doing vibes duets with Terry Gibbs, but never got the recognition she deserved because she insisted on staying home with her family!

Dorothy Ashby, a Jazz *harpist* from Detroit. Ms. Ashby has written a book on modern harmony for Jazz harp and cello!

Melba Liston (1926-), the only first-rate female trombonist in Jazz, grew up in L.A., played with Basie, Diz, Billie Holiday, and Quincy Jones—and even had bit parts in a couple of movies!

Norma Carson, a talented trumpet player inspired by Diz and Miles, who free-lanced around Philadelphis from the 50s on.

Patti Bown, a powerful pianist who toured with Quincy Jones.

Shirley Scott, an organist who records with husband Stanley Turrentine, a good tenor sax player who plays too much R & B.

...and others too few to mention.

Two contemporary Jazzwomen who draw rave reviews from members of all twelve sexes are **Geri Allen** and **Cassandra Wilson** but we'll save them for the section on New Jazz.

Jazz Singers

If women have been drastically underrepresented as instrumental Jazz musicians, as singers they've been at the forefront of Jazz. The roots of Jazz singing can be traced back to **Bessie Smith, Ma Rainey**, and **Clara Smith**. Although these women are considered *Blues* singers, they recorded their best work with Jazz musicians.

They were followed by **Little Jimmy Rushing** (1902-72), who worked almost entirely in Jazz (mainly with the Count Basie band), and the huge-voiced **Big Joe Turner** (1911-85) who, tried his mighty tonsils on damn near everything, including rock'n'roll.

However (sorry to be redundant), *real* Jazz singing pretty much began with **Louis Armstrong**. Pops reinvented Jazz vocals just about as drastically as he had revolutionized improvised Jazz solos. He applied the same principles of rewriting the melody, bending phrases, and multiplying the rhythm as he had in his trumpet solos. He also invented **"scat"** singing, the "deconstruction" of a song's lyrics into nonsense sylla-

DID YOU KNOW...?

Joya Sherrill, a singer / songwriter who worked briefly with Duke Ellington, wrote the lyrics to Strayhorn / Ellington's famous "Take the A Train" while she was still in high-school.

bles—which a good scat singer could make more meaningful than "real" words.

Don't be fooled by his old-fashioned manner. Mr. Armstrong was a power-house—one of the true geniuses of the 20th century.

MUSICAL STRUCTURALISM...?

Modern linguists ("structural-ists") have a theory that is interesting and beautiful despite its hideous origin.

It goes like this: Captives from many different African cultures were thrown together in America; they had no common language, so they made up words—"pidgin English"—the beginning of a new language; at first the words had no grammar (no logical way to hook them together); the grammar didn't develop gradually, as you'd expect; the grammar was invented whole by the first generation of newborn chil-dren—because language is built-in to the marvellous structure of the human mind. (Bellcurved Genetic Racists take note: these "mar-vellous human minds" belonged to African people!)

Which set me to wondering...

If language is built-in to the human mind, why not music? Don't the facts indicate, imply, insist, scream out that the "grammar" of Jazz was born fully grown into the body / soul / mind / spirit of Louis Armstrong?

Jazz singing branched out in different directions after Louis.

Witty **Fats Waller** mocked a song by smartassing its lyrics.

Billie Holiday did the opposite—she went inside the song, straight to its heartbeat, and magnified its meaning. The instrumental parts of her singing—the authority with which she dragged a phrase or bent a melody—were exemplary, but Billie's real power lay in the emotion and inti-macy she brought to even the dumbest popular songs. Billie didn't just change Jazz singing, she changed popular singing, period.

HEIRS TO THE THRONE

Ella Fitzgerald (1918-) and **Sarah Vaughn** (1924-1990) sang Jazz and Pop and everything in between. Ella, especially when she was young, bubbled and swung. She hit it big with her infectious 1938 recording of "A Tisket, A Tasket." She recorded until 1989 when, after 50 years of singing, her voice was still in decent shape. For some tastes, Ella was rather bland, but she was so good and so musically unpretentious that you had to like her.

Sarah Vaughn was another story: Sarah's singing was much showier than Ella's—and she was more of a Jazz singer. Some people thought she was the greatest; others accused her of using too much pointless coloratura (opera term meaning "outrageously fancy stuff"). Check out a record she made with Billy Eckstine, "Dedicated to You." I'm not sure that it's Jazz, but it's as beautiful a voice as has ever decorated the earth.

DID YOU KNOW?

Compared to, say, Bessie Smith's rafter-rattlin' voice, Billie Holiday's voice was a mere whisper. Beautifully nuanced, and intimate as it was, Billie's voice would have been unimpressive without the invention of the microphone.

SCAT AND VOCALESE

A few people (like bop singer Babs Gonzalez) specialized in scat singing but for the most part, scat singing is just something that Jazz singers do. (Both Ella and Sarah were good at it.)

"**Vocalese**" is scat singing in reverse: you take the notes of an

improvised Jazz solo, then put words to it. A famous example is King Pleasure's "Moody's Mood for Love." It's great fun, and in some backdoor way it teaches you how Jazz solos work.

Lambert, Hendricks, & Ross, an accomplished "Vocalese" trio—is amazing in small doses. Ditto for Manhattan Transfer, their successors.

Back to women singers: Carmen McRae (1922-94) is a respected singer who many think should be

more famous. Ms. McRae sings with great intelligence, impeccable musicality, and little emotion.

She is not, however, one of the Cool School. The founding mother of the Cool School was Anita O'Day (1919-), who was twice as good (but only half as cool) as her desciples, June Christy (1926-90) and Chris Connor (1929-). O'Day was rhythmic, smart, and full of musical surprises.

Another fine singer, **Nina Simone** (1933-), is *much different* than Billie Holiday but comes close to Billie's emotional intensity. Ms. Simone was born in North Carolina, escaped to Philadelphia, did time at Julliard, and spent four years accompanying other singers. (She's a good pianist.) In 1959 she hit it big with her recording of "Porgy," and she's been strong ever since.

"Aren't there any MALE Jazz Singers?"
Yes, of course...but nobody's sure who they are!

Billy Eckstine, sometimes referred to as a Jazz singer, was the first black male singer to be a big hit with white dudes.

Joe Williams is a Blues singer. Or Jazz singer. Or both? (Whatever the hell he is, he's good!)

Al Jarreau and **Bobby McFerrin** are contemporary scat (and-then-some) singers who've extended the form. Jarreau did the theme song ("...we met on the wayyyyyy.") for the TV series "Moonlighting." McFerrin's version of "Round Midnight" was featured in the award-winning film of the same name.

Leon Thomas' African-inspired "yodeling" was arguably <u>the</u> singing innovation of the lively 70s. **Johnny Hartman**\, called "the most underrated Jazz singer in the world," is an acquired taste (that I've never acquired). (My nominee for "the most underrated" is a guy named **Bill Henderson** who you've probably never heard of. Too bad for ya.)

A few men and women who, whether they're Jazz singers or not, certainly deserve a mention are: **Dinah Washington, Dakota Staton, Abbey Lincoln, Cleo Laine, Nancy Wilson, Low Rawls, Mel Torme, Jackie Paris, Bobby Short, Miriam Makeba, Anita Baker...** and a cast of thousands.

Is Jazz singing Important?

Yes.

Why?

Because most people get into Jazz by listening first to Jazz singers, then to Jazz instrumentalists.

Who Is/Isn't a Jazz Singer?

Some people think Nina Simone isn't a Jazz singer, and some people think Frank Sinatra is. It doesn't matter. All that matters is that you listen to the music. (You can call a giraffe an elephant if it pleases you... just keep listening.

1980s & 90s
HipHop &
Young Fogeys
(...is Jazz d-e-a-d?)

A few years ago a Time magazine cover story announced the "Death of the Age of Selfishness." The last six times I looked, more people lived on the streets, fewer people had jobs, and selfishness seemed to be healthier every year.

So when a 1990 Time cover featured young Jazz trumpeter Wynton Marsalis alongside a headline proclaiming "The New Jazz Age," my immediate reaction was: You'd better call a priest.

WHAT's THE REAL SITUATION?

In many ways, Jazz has evolved through the same stages as European classical music, with the result that Jazz, like classical music, has "progressed" itself into a corner. And, Jazz, like classical music, has been trying to work its way out of that corner by going backward and forward at the same time.

> **Backward** = exploring its own history
> **Forward** = trying every new trick imaginable—new Fusions, new blood (transFusions?), new ideas, serencipity (happy accidents) ...and..."Ingredient X"

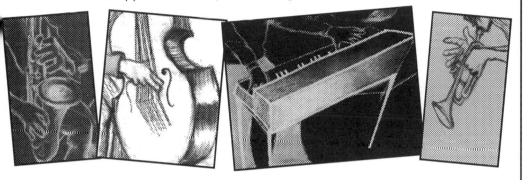

EXPLORING ITS OWN HISTORY?

What does that mean, Exploring its own history?

> In theory, it can mean a lot of things.

> In practice, it usually means that a player puts himself back at some earlier stage of Jazz, either because he simply loves the music or because he feels—or wonders—what if Jazz had done this instead of that?.

You go back to that place where, to you, the music was still ... coming from God. You can stay there forever, or you can wait for the forks in the road and take them your way.

THE YOUNG FOGEYS

Some of the first players to turn to Jazz history for inspiration were Scott Hamilton (sax) and Warren Vache (cornet)—but the real stars of Young Fogeydom are, of course, The Brothers...

THE BROTHERS

Wynton and **Branford Marsalis**, New Orleans-born brothers (in both senses of the word) came on the scene in the 80s.

Wynton, a dazzling trumpet technician, headed what critics like to call a "neo-classical" Jazz movement. He started at Bebop and worked his way backward into the grinning lap of Dixieland.

and worked his way backward into the grinning lap of Dixieland.

(Don't be alarmed by that going backward. Some of history's greatest advances—the Renaissance, for one—were made by men who started by going backwards: "Renaissance" means "revival'''' they thought they were going back to ancient Greece.)

Wynton not only investigated all of Jazz for his roots—and his Voice—he also blew the hell out of some classical trumpet.

My nomination for most far-out Fusion: Wynton cut a record with opera egodiva Kathleen Battle (talk about Bitches Brew)!

As of early 1995, Wynton and Bradford are still going strong:

Branford Marsalis leads the orchestra on the Jay Leno Tonight Show. (Branford is so witty and likeable that they should let him host the Tonight Show and let Leno lead the band.)

Wynton Marsalis has created—and presides over—a Lincoln Center Jazz Orchestra, giving Jazz a legitimacy that it has long deserved. (That's a mixed blessing: Jazz's ascendance to the status of African-American Classical Music reinforces the feeling that Jazz is now "museum music" like the European Classics.)

CHARISMA (OR THE LACK THEREOF)

In Jazz, you always have the feeling that if the right player comes along—another Bird, a new Coltrane, or some weird new thang (Miles Pavarotti?)—the music could change the world.

Despite his virtuousity, Wynton leaves a lot of people cold. Maybe he should dress up like Cher or

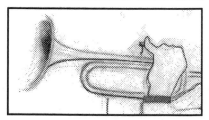

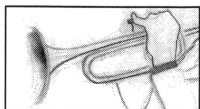

have someone step on his trumpet or let Dennis Rodman do his hair? Wynton doesn't seem to have the flair to lead the Jazzraelitss out of bondage. Maybe he'll surprise us. Maybe it'll be one of the Jazzy HipHoppers.

FUSION: HIPHOP & HERBIE THE HOMEBOY

Ever since Miles fused Jazz with Rock, Jazzdudes have looked to mate with young people's music. The main youth music that Jazz tried fusing with in the late 80s and early 90s is HipHop. Jazz-HipHop Fusion has been tried by both older and younger guys. Miles tried it before he died. (Maybe that's what killed him?)

Herbie Hancock—younger than Miles, older than "indigenous" HipHoppers—tried it. (The music wasn't great, but Herbie's argument with Wynton Marsalis was. Later.)

The younger groups like M-Base fared better.

STOP!

I Repeat: "Is Jazz D-E-A-D?"

If d-e-a-d means Not selling any records, then Jazz is okay. (Not great but okay.) If d-e-a-d means Without a direction—without a Miles or a Bird or a Trane, well ...

"...there are no young rebels... we don't even have a charlatan."
--Henry Threadgill, avant garde Jazzman, *DOWNBEAT MAGAZINE*

But hey ... Jazz and the novel have died more times than the troubled young dude in the Halloween hockey mask. (The minute you turn your back, they're sneaking around behind you with a meat cleaver!)

The problem is not that Jazz is dead, the problem is... The problem is...that we are so...

We live in a time without passionate direction...

"The best lack all conviction, while the worst
Are full of passionate intensity.
Surely some revelation is at hand...."

Jazz will have a direction when we have a direction.
Jazz will become vital when we become vital.
Jazz will be creative when we become creative.

Meanwhile, we'll have to look in other places
for a Bird or a Miles or a Coltrane
to light the Sacred Fire.

Like..?

Like...

Maybe we're looking on the wrong side of the gender gap.

Maybe it's a *Joan* Coltrane or a *Sinead* Bechet that Jazz needs. Every other art form (including sex) has benefitted from the inclusion of women. Women have changed everything from fiction to movies to men. So why not Jazz?

A couple absolutely asskickin' young pianists, Geri Allen and Joanne Brackeen, have already started. In the words of John Fordham: **"Allen emerged as a virtuoso performer, mingling the rich keyboard voicing of Bill Evans with steely resolve and Monklike truculence."**

(Monklike truculence, huh?)

LIKE...

Maybe one of the HipHopping young-bloods has the key.

New York's M-Base collective—especially sax players **Gary Thomas** and **Greg Osby** —combine Jazz with HipHop and other new black dance music in ways that don't seem condescending.

The only Jazz singer who's come close to "BeBop" Betty Carter is "HipHop" **Cassandra Wilson**, the ferocious vocalist who started out with M-Base in the 80s but now flies on her own.

Sax player **Steve Coleman**, whether with his band the Five Elements, or backing Ms. Wilson, is a powerful improviser who likes Funky rhythm shifts where mere Earthlings use melody.

WORLD FUSION...

The world is shrinking, the borders are weeping: Europe is Japan is Africa is Australia is Harlem...highbrow art is merging with middlebrow, lowbrow, nobrow, your mama's eyebrow...

• A London orchestra, Loose Tubes, mixes everything but Arafat's hat into compositions by pianist **Django Bates**.

• British saxophonist **Courtney Pine** (he's the one who turned 30!) mixes Coltrane, African pop, and reggae.

• Scandanavian sax player **Jan Garbarek** mixes Coltrane with Norwegian cattle calls. (Did you say Cattle calls???)

• Brazilian saxophonist **Gato Barbieri**, last I heard, was still fusing free Jazz and Brazilian...orgasms.

• South African pianist **Abdullah Ibrahim** has been fusing African music with Jazz since the 60s, and he's still going.

• ...and somewhere out there, **Sun Ra** was fusing (or trying his damndest to fuse) the Twelve Apostles with the Three Stooges. (Saint Larry, Curly, and Moe?)

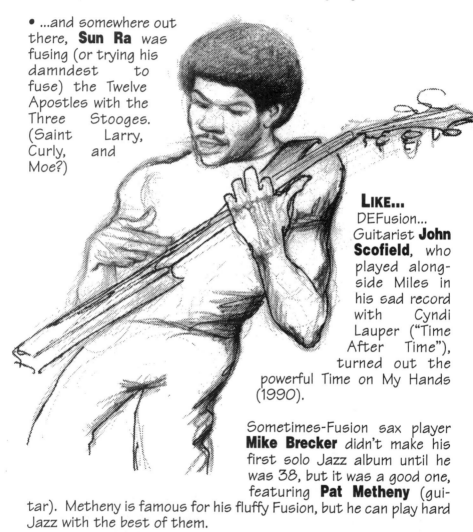

LIKE...
DEFusion... Guitarist **John Scofield**, who played alongside Miles in his sad record with Cyndi Lauper ("Time After Time"), turned out the powerful Time on My Hands (1990).

Sometimes-Fusion sax player **Mike Brecker** didn't make his first solo Jazz album until he was 38, but it was a good one, featuring **Pat Metheny** (guitar). Metheny is famous for his fluffy Fusion, but he can play hard Jazz with the best of them.

And **Keith Jarrett**, the Princess Di of defusers? What does Keithy have up his sleeve? I can't wait to see. I mean hear!

LIKE...
Freer Free Jazz...

The Free Jazz movement of the 60s & 70s had a more lasting impact in Europe than it did in The States. In Europe, Free Jazz became so free that nobody knows what to call it! Some of the best European musicians still play free Wha-cha-ma-call-it.

Cecil Taylor, one of the grandaddy's of the avant garde, is still at it, inspiring some people and pissing off others.

LIKE...
Reincarnation...

I'm not smilng; I'm serious. Jazz is the only sport where they reincarnate you while you're still alive! If you think I'm joking...

• The athletic approach of Dizzy Gillespie passed to **Jon Faddis** ten years before Diz himself passed!

• Bud Powell was reincarnated 20 times before he turned 30!

• By the end of Miles' career, **Wallace Roney** did Miles better than Miles.

• (...and that movie about all the Charlie Parker reincarnos...The Birds?)

You want to hear something that isn't impossible? One of these days, some Holy Fool will come along who is trying his damnedest to impersonate Miles, Bird, Coltrane, whoever... and that Sacred Bonehead will be playing God's music without even knowing it! It'll happen -- I'm fifteen percent certain of it!

(I don't know about you, but until that Sacred Bonehead comes along, I would rather hear Wallace Roney's Miles than the Miles who played next to Cindi Lauper.)

LIKE...

Maybe it's time for GrownUps to take the responsibility for making Jazz a living and vital art instead of trying to infuse Jazz with false vitality by tagging along with the latest teenage fad.

Miles Davis, as much as I loved his music, set a precedent for sucking up to teenagers that is shrinking Jazz to this day. Jazz is smart music—African-American classical music—but as long as Jazz's standards are set by teenagers, naive music will win out over smart music every time.

...so maybe it's time for GrownUps like Gato Barbieri, Carla Bley, Hamiet Bluiett, Anthony Braxton, Donald Byrd, Betty Carter, Don Cherry, Ornette Coleman, Steve Coleman, Alice Coltrane, Chick Corea, Jack DeJohnette, Paco DeLucia, Art Farmer, Jan Garbarek, Charlie Haden, Herbie Hancock, John Handy, Joe Henderson, Andrew Hill, Freddie Hubbard, Bobby Hutcherson, Abdullah Ibrahim, Keith Jarrett, Elvin Jones, Quincy Jones, Charles Lloyd, John MacLaughlin, Jackie McLean, Pat Metheny, Gerry Mulligan, Courtney Pine (you're over 30, baby!), Sam Rivers, Pharoah Sanders, Archie Shepp, Wayne Shorter, John Surman, Cecil Taylor, Leon Thomas, McCoy Tyner, Tony WIlliams and all those other utterly brilliant Jazz gentlemen and lades to show the teeny-boppers what Jazz is all about.

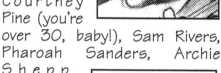

LIKE...
Ask **Phyllis Lodge**
The BIGGG Question.

Phyllis Lodge is presently writing a biography of **McCoy Tyner** (Passion Dance -- a Journey through the Piano Music of McCoy Tyner), the powerhouse pianist who blasted his way to  fame in John Coltrane's legendary 1960 quartet—and since then, has been one of the strongest forces in Jazz.

Little Question

Ron: *Jazz isn't dead, is it? I can handle the truth.*
Phyllis: No (laughing), it's just in a sort of nebulous period. But there are good signs.

Little Question

Ron: *Like?*
Phyllis: Like women—a couple of good up-and-coming saxophone players in Chicago. And Geri Allen—I think she teaches at Howard—the girl is brilliant! Geri Allen! And McCoy.

BIGGG Question

Ron: *If there was one thing Jazz could do to get itself out of this "nebulous period"...what would it be?*
Phyllis: If there was only one thing...I'd say that the musicians have to play together. The worst thing about the situation we have now is that the musicians don't play together. Groups are put together by the people handling the money. You have a group that lasts for a few days or a week, and that's it. There's no interplay. Musicians have to play together so they can feed off each other and get excited by each other's ideas.

(Amen.)

This is a book on music, not on race. But the fact is that America has tried to minimize the crime against Africa and its people by pretending that Africa was a country devoid of civilization, filled with savages. That, of course, is a lie.

> "Who controls the past controls the future;
> who controls the present controls the past."
> -- from "1984" by George Orwell

The Olduvai Gorge was the place where human beings first appeared.

Archaeological evidence of advanced civilizations going back thousands of years has been found all over Africa. The Egyptians

—Africans—were more civilized in 4000 BC than Europeans were until well after the Renaissance.

The slave traders who decimated Africa didn't destroy "primitive" cultures—which would have been disgusting enough—they destroyed entire civilizations...

...which brings us back to the question we started with...

What is Jazz?
⊷ part 2

Civilizations are one thing.
Human beings are another.

HUMAN BEINGS
How many Jewish human beings were killed in the Jewish Holocaust? Virtually anyone, anywhere will say, "Six million." That is how emblazoned it is in the world's conscience.

Now...how many black human beings were killed in the Black Holocaust —from the start of the European slave trade [c.1500] to the abolition of slavery in the U.S. [c.1862]?

THE TRUTH?
People with PhDs say everything from two million to 150 million!

A major economic event for Europe and Asia, a near fatal event for Africa, the seminal event in the history of every African American— if not every American!—and it barely exists in our consciousness as anything real, solid, or factual. Just a free-floating sense of rage or self-pity on one side and a vague mix of guilt, indifference and denial on the other.

What is the truth?

This is as close to the truth as I've been able to find.
(When in doubt, I have understated.)

**The total number of slaves imported is not known.
It is estimated that nearly 900,000 came to America in the
sixteenth century, 2.75 million in the seventeenth century, 7
million in the eighteenth, and over 4 million in the nineteenth
— perhaps 15 million in total.**

**Probably every slave imported represented,
on the average, five corpses in Africa or on the high seas.
The American slave trade, therefore, meant the elimination
of at least 60 million Africans
-- from "The Black Triangle" by Armet Francis**

The death of 60 million Africans? (Sixty MILLION?)

That struck me as so astonishing that I asked S.E. Anderson, author of The Black Holocaust for Beginners. "After all the research you've done, what's your best estimate of the number of Africans killed during the Black Holocaust?"

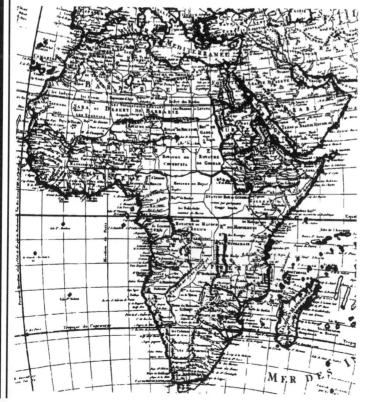

"Conservative estimate—at least 50 million."

Conservative estimate—at least 50 million—nearly ten times the number killed in the Jewish Holocaust?

Am I the only person in America who didn't know that?

Don't get me wrong: We should not minimize the Jewish Holocaust. We should make books, movies, museums, and memorials to document the Jewish Holocaust.

We should do everything humanly possible to honor the dead, to protect the living, and to prevent it from ever happening again.

> But the people of Africa that our own country murdered?
> FIFTY to SIXTY million of them?
> (And the fifteen million it enslaved?)
> That blood. That anguish. The love that can't be expressed.
> (And the children?)

People that I love have awakened in the middle of the night when a person they loved died thousands of miles away. If one dying person can do that, what can fifty million do?

How many of us have been reduced to anguished convulsions when we visited Dachau or one of the other concentration camps? Isn't there some sense in which memorials to the Holocaust are not the work of the living, but the cry of the six million dead?

BITS & PIECES:

"I was much disturbed by his music. Here was a creative person who had become a vegetarian, who was studying yoga and reading the Bhagavad-Gita, yet in whose music I still hear much turmoil."
-- Ravi Shankar on John Coltrane

"What did he tell that audience? In what new and meaningful things did his music instruct them?"
-- Martin Williams on John Coltrane

"It sounds like a man strapped down...screaming to be free."
-- A psychiatrist on John Coltrane

"Miles Davis plays it with a stark, deeply felt communal anguish that jazz has not heard since King Oliver."
-- Martin Williams on Miles Davis

I believe that Jazz, in some way that I don't begin to understand, is the cry of anguish of the millions of African human beings whose murder we have never acknowledged, whose deaths we have never mourned, and whose blood screams at us across oceans, across time...

And this...

After emancipation...all those people who had been slaves, they needed the music more than ever now; it was like they were trying to find out in this music what they were supposed to do with this freedom: playing the music and listening to it—waiting for it to express what they needed to learn once they had learned it wasn't just white people the music had to reach to, nor even to their own people, but straight out to life, and to what a man does with his life when it finally is his.

Sidney Bechet
from his autobiography, Treat It Gentle...

Biographies

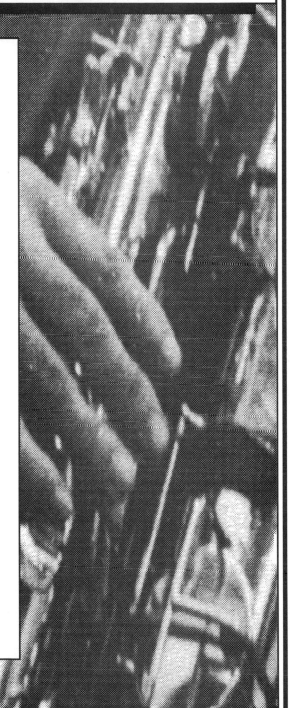

1. Scott Joplin
2. Buddy Bolden
3. Jelly Roll Morton
4. Louis Armstrong
5. Sidney Bechet
6. Bix Beiderbecke
7. Duke Ellington
8. Benny Goodman
9. Count Basie
10. Coleman Hawkins
11. Lester Young
12. Billie Holiday
13. Charlie Parker
14. Dizzy Gillespie
15. Thelonious Monk
16. Bud Powell
17. Max Roach
18. Charles Mingus
19. Sonny Rollins
20. Miles Davis
21. John Coltrane
22. Ornette Coleman
23. Eric Dolphy
24. Betty Carter
25. Keith Jarrett

Scott Joplin was the son of a former slave. Even as a child, there was no mistaking his genius, so his mother worked as a maid to pay for Scott's musical education. When she died, teenage Scott began travelling, studying, and performing. He wound up at George Smith College for Negroes in Sedalia, Missouri, where he began writing songs. His songs were so popular that they earned him the title King of Ragtime.

Scott Joplin

Pianist and Composer

b. 11 / 24 / 1868, Texas
d. 4 / 11 / 1917, New York City

Joplin wanted his music in concert halls, so he wrote ballets and operas -- in Ragtime!

That didn't satisfy the ambitious Mr. Joplin. Ragtime was considered lowlife music. Joplin wanted his music in concert halls, so he wrote ballets and operas—in Ragtime! His masterpiece—several years in the writing—was Treemonisha, a grand opera. People had bought up his rags as fast as he'd write them, but nobody of any color was interested in his opera—three hours of black consciousness-raising presented in a white middle-class fat lady art form!

In 1915, Joplin rented a Harlem theater and staged Treemonisha himself. No costumes, no scenery, no musicians other than Joplin himself on piano. It was a disaster. Joplin had a breakdown and died in a mental hospital a couple years later (1917). In 1972, Treemonisha was performed on Broadway, and Scott Joplin won a Pulitzer Prize for his contribution to American music.

Buddy
Bolden

The person most often credited with "inventing" Jazz is black barber, scandal sheet publisher, ladies' man, and cornettist **Buddy Bolden**. Since Buddy's career was over before the first Jazz recordings were made, all we

Cornettist and Bandleader

b. 1868, New Orleans
d. 11 / 4 / 1931, New Orleans

> **Buddy's band featured a repetoire that included a mix of popular dance tunes, a rough ensemble version of ragtime**

have left of him is legend. But it's quite a legend: Buddy was famous for his big bold cornet sound, his big bold personality, and his fierce blues playing, but he probably stayed closer to ragtime than to full-fledged Jazz. By all accounts, Buddy's band was playing ragtime with improvised embellishments by the late 1890s. Maybe I should say Buddy's bands, because legend has it that he was so popular that he had six or seven bands going in the same night, and he'd rush from one to the other.

His band featured cornet, clarinet, valve trombone, guitar, double bass, and drums. Its repetoire included a mix of popular dance tunes, a rough ensemble version of ragtime, and blues.

By the turn of the century many New Orleans bands had begun playing in the collective improvisational style pioneered by Buddy. One of those groups was the Original Dixieland Jazz Band, the group that made the first ever Jazz recording (1917).

In 1906, Buddy began suffering periods of derangement. In 1907, after running amok in the streets of New Orleans, Buddy was committed to a mental hospital, where he stayed for the last 24 years of his life.

Ferdinand Morton, the black sheep of a respectable New Orleans Creole family, started out playing in street parades and worked his way up into the gambling joints and ho-houses. He wore a diamond in his front tooth, was as ostentatiously insincere as a snake oil salesman, and claimed to have invented everything from the blues to Jazz:

One of his last recordings was "Mamie's Blues" (1939), which he introduces as "no doubt the first blues I heard in my life," and sings beautifully—sounding roughly as Humphrey Bogart might have done had he taken to blues singing. -- From JAZZ—the essential CD guide by Martin Gayford

Pianist / Composer/
Singer / Bandleader /
Boxing Promoter / Pimp

b. 10 / 20 / 1890, New
Orleans
d. 7 / 10 / 1941, Los Angeles

Jelly Roll's 1926 recordings as the leader of the Red Hot Peppers marked him as a great innovator as both soloist and bandleader. Ragtime, for all its charm, was a stiff and formal music. As a solo pianist, Morton loosened up its tidy rhythms and messed up its hair. As a band-

Jelly Roll Morton

leader, he gave the Jazz group an identity; he saw the group as a whole instead of a bunch of soloists.

Morton was doing all right until the mid-30s, when big band Swing wiped out all the competition. Jelly, obscure, broke, and never all that stable to begin with, got terminally pissed off when his song "King Porter Stomp" became a big hit—for Benny Goodman!—so Jelly Roll wrote a letter to the press declaring that he, Jelly Roll Morton, had invented Jazz!

That got the attention of academic/Jazz critic Alan Lomax, who recorded hours of Morton's music and highly fictionalized "autobiography" for the Library of Congress. Jelly Roll died in 1941, certain he had been cursed by his voodoo godmother.

Louis' recordings with his Hot Five are considered some of the glories of Jazz.

Louis Armstrong grew up in Storyville, the red-light district of New Orleans. His mother was a part-time prostitute; his father deserted her after the boy was

Louis
Armstrong

born. At age 12, Louis was put in the Colored Waif's Home, where he joined his first band. By 1919, Louis was playing cornet for Kid Ory, who ran the best Jazz band in New Orleans.

Trumpet and Vocals

b. 7 / 4 / 1900, New Orleans
d. 7 / 6 / 1971, New York City

To anyone who's been around Jazz awhile, the improvised Jazz solo seems like the ocean—something natural—so it's surprising to learn that someone had to invent it. When you learn that the inventor was Louis Armstrong—the man who grinned?—wow!

By 1922, nobody had ever heard anything like the solos Louis was playing. He was invited to Chicago to play for King Oliver, whose Creole Jazz Band was the best Jazz band in the world.

Within five years Louis Armstrong transformed Jazz.

(That's a hell of a resume!)

In 1925 he embarked on the series of recordings with his Hot Five, that are considered some of the glories of Jazz. In 1929, with pianist Earl Hines, Lewis recorded his masterpiece, "West End Blues."

Somewhere during the 1930s, Louis Armstrong became "Satchmo," the grinning, singing entertainer. He was so good at being Satchmo that it may never have occurred to you to wonder what he'd been before. This story will give you a taste:

Some of the top guns of the Boston Symphony Orchestra had heard rumors of genius, but they were skeptical, so they went to check it out for themselves. They stopped by Louis's dressing room and asked him to play something...

Louis picked up his horn and obliged, performing the requested passage and then improvising a dazzling stream of variations. Shaking their heads, these "legitimate" trumpet players left the room, one of them saying, "I watched his fingers and I still don't know how he does it. I also don't know how it is that, playing there all by himself, he sounded as if a whole orchestra were behind him. I never heard a musician like this...I thought he was just a colored entertainer."
--from Jazz Is by Nat Hentoff

As a child **Sidney Bechet** taught himself the clarinet, sat in with Freddie Keppard, and joined a marching band. In 1917, he joined black composer Will Marion Cook's Southern Syncopated Orchestra and toured Europe. Swiss conductor Ernest Ansermet called Sidney an "extraordinary clarinet virtuoso... [an] artist of genius." Bechet was 22 at the time.

During the trip to Europe, Bechet discovered the soprano sax, and it became his main instrument. After he returned to the States, he played with some

Sidney
Bechet

top bands (including Duke Ellington's), but he was an ornery old cuss (even when he was young) who preferred the freedom of small groups. He made fine recordings in 1932 with The New Orleans Feetwarmers but the Depression brought his career to a screeching halt until 1939 when the Blue Note record company resurrected him for a spectacular recording of "Summertime."

Sidney played at the 1949 Paris Jazz Festival with Charlie Parker. He liked it so much that he stayed in Paris.

In much the same sense that Louis Armstrong "invented" the Jazz cornet and trumpet, Sydney Bechet invented the Jazz clarinet and soprano saxophone. When that new master of the soprano sax, John Coltrane, heard Sidney, he said, "Did all those old guys Swing like that?"

Clarinet and Soprano Saxophone

b. 5 / 14 / 1897, New Orleans
d. 5 / 14 / 1959, Paris

Although Bechet played with some of the top bands of his time, he was ornery and preferred the freedom of small groups.

Leon Bismarck Beiderbecke was the first great white Jazz player. Bix's middle-class parents wanted him to have a respectable profession, but Bix loved Jazz. His parents tried to straighten him out by sending him to a military academy near Chicago, but in 1922—the year Louis Armstrong moved to Chicago—Bix was expelled from school. When he heard Louis:

- Bix realized that he was in the presence of genius;
- Bix heard not only what Louis played, but what his playing implied;

Bix
Beiderbecke

Cornet

b. 3 / 10 / 1903, Iowa
d. 8 / 7 / 1931, New York City

> ***Bix developed his own tone, which "sounded like a girl saying yes."***

- Bix knew that he couldn't copy Louis—he had to find his own way.

By 1924, Bix had his own band, the Wolverines, and had developed a style all his own: his tone "sounded like a girl saying yes"; his improvisations (like Louis's) were basically songs-within-a-song, based on the original melody, but, where Armstrong's solos were hot and fierce, Bix's were intimate, cool. Bix's best recordings were made with saxophonist Frankie Trumbauer in 1927, around Bix's 24th birthday. At age 25, he joined Paul Whiteman's band.

Bix Beiderbecke may have been the first great white Jazz player, but his whitness couldn't protect him from the fate that struck down so many great black Jazzmen. Bix, dying from alcoholism and pneumonia, went to see his parents; he discovered that they'd never even opened the records he'd been sending them. Bix Beiderbecke died in a New York boarding house a few months later at the age of 28.

Duke
Ellington

Edward Kennedy Ellington was born to a middle-class black Washington family. His father was an ambitious valet; his mother was "real Victorian lady." Duke himself was handsome, witty, intelligent, suave, and confident. (Except for that, he didn't have a damned thing going for him.) He started out to be an artist, but by the time he was 30, he was leading an orchestra at New York's legendary Cotton Club. Ellington's approach to the big band was revolutionary:

Pianist / Composer / Bandleader

b. 4/29/1899, Washington D.C.
d. 5/24/1974, New York City

Before Duke, Jazz musicians wrote or orchestrated songs. Ellington used longer, more symphonic forms on Jazz material.

And Duke didn't write and arrange for instruments, but for individuals. In the words of Duke's co-composer/arranger Billy Strayhorn: "Ellington plays the piano, but his real instrument is his band. Each member of the band is to him a distinctive play of tone colors and a distinctive set of emotions."

Through 50 years of almost nonstop creativity and growth, Ellington showcased some of Jazz's greatest artists (from Sidney Bechet to Johnny Hodges) and wrote/cowrote thousands of compositions, including some of America's most distinctive songs (from "Mood Indigo" to "Take the A Train").

Benny Goodman was another of Jazz's prodigies. He was one of twelve children from an Eastern European Jewish family, whose talents were seen by his father as the family's ticket out of the ghetto. Benny was playing the clarinet around Chicago while he was still wearing short pants. He was a full-time pro by the time he was 14.

Benny Goodman

Clarinet and Bandleader

b. 5 / 30 / 1909, Chicago
d. 6 / 13 / 1986, New York City

Goodman's small Jazz groups were among the first to combine black and white musicians.

As a soloist, critics divide Goodman's career in two. During the early part of his career, Benny played with more emotion and less technique. By the mid-30s, he had developed the silky, technically spectacular style that made him famous. With the help of radio broadcasts and his celebrated 1935 tour, Benny Goodman started the craze for big band "Swing."

As a bandleader, Benny was like a Marine Drill Sergeant. His bands were so well "drilled" that most of his musicians couldn't stand him. On the other hand, Goodman's small Jazz groups were among the first to combine black and white musicians. His 1935 trio featured Goodman, pianist Teddy Wilson and the furiously energetic drummer (and showman) Gene Krupa. The addition of vibes player Lionel Hampton, guitarist Charlie Christian, and trumpeter Cootie Williams resulted in the Benny Goodman Sextet 1940-41, which was the musical highpoint of Benny's career, although he put together bands and small groups until his death in 1986.

William Count Basie doesn't fit neatly into the history of Jazz. Like Ellington, Basie started out as a stride pianist, but Ellington's piano style never had much influence; Basie's did. After a stint pianoing for silent movies, Basie wound up with Bennie Moten's fine Kansas City band. After Moten died in

Count
Basie

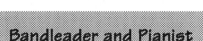

Bandleader and Pianist

b. 8 / 21 / 1904, Red Bank,
New Jersey
d. 4 / 26 / 1984, Florida

1935, Basie became the bandleader and brought the band, filled with the best musicians in the Southwest, to New York. By then, Basie's piano playing had become a sort of "minimalist stride." Like Miles and Monk would do later, Basie's solos were filled with large silent spaces.

The band had great energy, great soloists (Lester Young, tenor sax; Buck Clayton, trumpet) and, thanks largely to the marvellous drummer Jo Jones, it swung.

Many big bands, including Basie's, went under after World War II, but by 1952 he was back with one of his best bands ever, featuring Thad Jones and Joe Newman on trumpets, Frank Foster and Eddie "Lockjaw" Davis on sax, and singer Joe Williams.

If you think you've never heard Count Basie, think again: virtuallly every Jazz or pop singer between 1950 and 1980—Ella Fitzgerald, Sarah Vaughn, Frank Sinatra, Tony Bennett, to name just a few—recorded with Basie. Basie had great bands in every decade from the 30s to the 70s but his only "hit" record was the goofy 1947 "Open the Door, Richard."

Virtually every Jazz or pop singer between 1950 and 1980 -- Ella, Sassy, Sinatra, Tony Bennett, -- recorded at one time with Count Basie's bands.

A few adventurous guys tried Jazz on the sax before **Coleman Hawkins,** but it was Hawk who made the saxophone the dominant Jazz instrument it is today. Hawkins, who came from a well-off family, studied the cello at an early age, then switched to the sax. A lifelong lover of classical music (especially opera), he was hip to conventional music theory.

By 1924, when Louis Armstrong arrived on the scene, Hawk was already the star of the Fletcher Henderson band. Whereas Armstrong had built his improvisations around melody. Hawkins based his own improvisations on rhythmic drive and harmony.

Coleman
Hawkins

Tenor Saxophone

b. 11 / 21 / 1904, St. Joe, MO
d. 4 / 19 / 1969, New York
City

Hawk's version of "Body and Soul" is the gold standard against which all other Jazz ballads are measured.

Hawk's mature styles—both of them—emerged in 1929, on two recordings: on the fast piece ("Hallo Lola"), his playing surged forward with great force and a flood of notes; on the slow piece ("One Hour), he became sensous and rhapsodic. (Hawkins is credited with inventing the Jazz ballad.) In 1934, Hawk went to Europe. He returned to The States in 1939 and made what is considered his recorded masterpiece—"Body and Soul"—the gold standard against which all other Jazz ballads are measured.

When Bop came on in the 1940s, Hawkins was one of its early supporters. He continued to record into the late 50s. His saxophone tone was still so powerful that one young player said to another that playing next to Hawk frightened him. "Coleman Hawkins," the other player said, "is supposed to frighten you."

Lester Young

Tenor Saxophone

b., 8 / 27 / 1909, Woodville, Miss.

d. 3 / 15 / 1959, New York City

Lester Young, the oldest of three children who played in the family's vaudeville band, quit after an argument with his father and went to Kansas City, one of the hotbeds of Jazz. In K.C., Lester played with King Oliver, Benny Moten, and the touring Fletcher Henderson band...

Jazz Mythology:
...one night Fletcher Henderson's tenor sax player—the legendary Coleman Hawkins—didn't show up for work. So Lester, considerate young dude that he was, sat in for him. Lester was so good that when Coleman Hawkins heard about him, Mr. Hawkins, tenor sax in hand, went looking for the young whippersnapper to teach him a lesson.

When the Hawk finally found Lester, as Wynton Marsalis puts it, "he wished he hadn't." They had a tenor sax shootout that lasted all night and half of the next morning. Not long after that, Mr. Hawkins went to Europe, and Lester replaced him in Fletcher Henderson's band.

That was in 1934. It should have been a happily-ever-after story, but it turned sour when Lester realized he was hired to play like Hawkins. Hawk was a real athlete on the tenor: he was fast and aggressive and his sound was huge! Lester played fewer notes, played with a softer tone, blurred them together. He didn't say, he implied (like Miles a few years later). Lester didn't mind replacing Hawkins, but damned if he'd impersonate him. Lester quit.

In 1936 he joined the Count Basie Band, where he stayed until 1949. Although Prez made his greatest recordings during the Basie years, he didn't make them all with Basie. During that period, Prez made a series of recordings with Billie Holiday. (Some sources say that she nicknamed him "Prez" and he baptized her "Lady Day." Other sources say that he when he smoked Coleman Hawkins, he became the Prez[ident]?) Together, Prez and Billie made some of the finest vocal/sax recordings in Jazz history. It was a collaboration of two slightly off-center geniuses.

Lester spent his last years in a room across the street from Birdland. The movie Round Midnight (1986) looks without sentimentality at Prez' alcoholism and dignity. Saxophonist Dexter Gordon, who had many of the same problems, was nominated for an Oscar for playing Prez.

Together, Prez and Billie Hollday made some of the finest vocal / sax recordings in Jazz history.

Billie Holiday is probably the only singer considered a great Jazz musician when judged by the standards you'd apply to Bird, Diz, Miles, and the boys in the band. (I will pause here while fans of Ella, Sarah, etc. curse me out.) But that only accounts for part of her fame. Thanks to her famous autobiography—and the movie—her life, her personality, her mythology, account for the rest. Her book, Lady Sings the Blues, starts like this:

"Mom and Pop were just a couple of kids when they got married. He was eighteen, she was sixteen, and I was three."

Billie
Holiday

Her musician father took off, and her mother went to New York to look for work, leaving Billie with relatives who took turns abusing her. Billie moved to New York, worked as a maid, then as a teenage hooker, then legend takes over:

They say that one night in 1930—Billie would have been about 15—to keep her mom from being evicted, Billie sang "Body and Soul" and reduced the audience to tears. If that sounds a little improbable, this is a fact: In 1933, Billie, 18 or 19, made her first recordings with Benny Goodman's band. In 1936, she cut several records with pianist Teddy Wilson that feature the first collaborations between Billie and tenor saxophonist Lester Young. If ever two people shared one musical soul, it was Billie and Lester. The recordings they made (scope out "He's Funny That Way," cut in 1938) are little miracles.

Singer

b. 4 / 7 / 1915, Baltimore
d. 7 / 17 / 1959, New York City

Billie's first recordings were made with Benny Goodman's band when she was 18 years old.

Billie's career went through three phases:

The first phase was the one mentioned above, one of the high points of which was her 1939 recording of "Strange Fruit," Lewis Allen's straight-ahead poem about lynchings.

The second was in the mid-40s, when Billie recorded with strings (including her own famous composition, "Don't Explain").

By the 50s—the third period—booze and heroin were ruining her voice, but the sensibility behind it was more moving than ever. Her 1958 Lady in Satin, sounded like her voice had died and come back to haunt us from the grave. (She was never more powerful.)

In music she had perfect instincts; in life she had the opposite. She fell in love with men who abused her, stole her money, played with other women, and introduced her to heroin.

In May 1959, a few months after the death of Lester Young, Billie collapsed. She died ten weeks later. To this day, an astonishing number of people, half of them middle-class white girls, identify with Billie Holiday, a self-advertised born victim. There's just something about her.

> # In music, Billie had perfect instincts; in life, she had the opposite.

Charlie Parker's father left when Bird was 11. His mother was so determined to make up for it that she worked two jobs while Charlie prowled Kansas City nightclubs and practiced Lester Young solos on the saxophone she'd bought him.

Little Charlie, a self-taught alto sax prodigy, didn't realize that Jazz in the 40s was played in only a few keys, so the obsessive little genius learned to play every song in every key by the time he'd reached his mid-teens. Without that "mistake," there might never have been any such thing as BeBop.

Charlie
Parker

Neat Coincidence: At about exactly the same time, French filmmaker Jean Cocteau (his "Beauty & the Beast" inspired the hairy TV series) remarked that new artists try to imitate the old masters, but they screw it up and their mistakes become the new masterpieces.

Alto Saxophone

b. 8 / 20 / 1920, Kansas City
d. 3 / 12 / 1955, New York City

Young Charlie quit school at fifteen to become a musician.

It was a brutal education: Once, still in his teens, Charlie was jamming in a Kansas City club, doing all right until he tried doing double tempo on Body and Soul. "Everybody fell out laughing. I went home and cried and didn't want to play again for three months." On another night, Bird sat in with Count Basie at the Reno Club. He started out fine, but fell out of key, couldn't find it again, then lost the time. Drummer Jo Jones stopped playing and threw one of his cymbals at Parker's feet. Bird, humiliated,

In 1945, Diz and Bird began the spectacular recordings that produced "Groovin' High," "Billie's Bounce," "Now's The Time," and "Ko-Ko."

packed up his horn and left the club.

When he turned up in Chicago a couple years later, Billy Eckstine described him as looking "like he just got off a freight car....but playing like you never heard—wailing alto." In New York, Bird washed dishes at Jimmy's Chicken Shack in Harlem so he could listen to Art Tatum's piano. Around that time, Bird experienced what he called "an epiphany." (An epiphany?)

Epiphany isn't a 9-to-5 word. It's a religious word meaning "a revelation of a divine being." In a more casual sense, an epiphany is a spiritual event in which The Answer to a Great Question is revealed in a sudden flash of knowing.

The most telling thing about the word "epiphany" used in an artistic (as opposed to religious) sense, is that it's a James Joyce word. Joyce, the Pope of experimental novelists, owns the word. Which means: 1) Bird knew Joyce's work; 2) Bird saw his own 'epiphany' in Joycean terms; 3) Bird, to some extent, identified with Joyce—a white, Irish novelist.

The Question: Was Bird, like Joyce, trying to "forge in the smithy of my soul, the uncreated conscience of my race?"

Bird's Epiphany: Charlie Parker was bored with the standard chord changes: "I kept thinking there's bound to be something else. I could hear it...but I couldn't play it." One night as he and guitarist Buddy Fleet were jamming at a chili house in Harlem, Bird realized in a sudden flash of knowing how to play what he'd been hearing!

Drummer Kenny Clark ('Klook') heard Bird at Monroe's Uptown House and was so dazzled that he brought Parker to Minton's and together, Dizzy, Bird, Klook and Monk reinvented Jazz.

In 1945, Diz and Bird began the spectacular recordings that produced "Grovin' High," "Billie's Bounce," "Now's the Time," and "Ko-Ko." Parker recorded six brilliant albums for Dial records, despite the fact that his mental and physical health were deteriorating. On the second Dial session, Parker could barely stay on his feet, but his playing was breathtaking. His rendition of "Lover Man" was one of the most stripped-bare, anguished Jazz performances of all time. It left little doubt about either his genius or his impending collapse.

With the help of impresario Norman Granz, Parker made some recordings with strings for Verve records. They weren't his best recordings, but they were better than they had any right to be.

Bird was a genius. And a heroin addict. They used to say, "If you want to play like Bird, you have to be like Bird." Of course, "Be," in that context meant, "Be a junkie." A lot of guys managed to be like Bird, but only one played like Bird.

"My candle burns from both ends, it will not last the night ...." Charlie Parker was as different from Edna St. Vincent Millay as you could get, but that line of hers fit him like a bodybag. In 1955, at the age of 34, Charlie Parker died. The examining physician said that Bird had the body of a 65-year-old man.

Bird was the paradigm of the Jazzman-as-victim.

Some say he was more the victim of himself than of society. To which Dizzy Gillespie would answer, "Where do you draw the line between the two if you're a black man?"

"My candle burns from both ends, it will not last the night..."

John Birks (Dizzy) Gillespie won a scholarship to South Carolina's Laurinburg Institute, where he learned to play both trumpet and piano. (In later years, Diz would adivse horn players to learn the piano, because it forced you to learn chords and harmony—and it was ideal for composing.)

Dizzy Gillespie

Diz, who loved a challenge, started out copying Roy Eldridge, the fastest, highest trumpeter around. Diz got so good that he replaced Eldridge in Teddy Hill's swing band when Roy left in 1937. Diz worked with Cab Calloway, the vocalist/bandleader who replaced Ellington at the Cotton Club, but Dizzy was too free-spirited for Calloway. They got in a wee fight (which Calloway later admitted was his own fault), and Cab fired Diz.

Diz, who'd had his fill of Calloway's "Heiddi ho" crap, had been searching for a more advanced kind of music. Like Bird, Diz could "hear" the new music in his head long before he could play it. In the 1940s Diz, Bird, Monk, Klook, Max Roach, Charlie Christian and a few others found each other and put together the pieces that each had developed on his own. The result was Bebop.

The recordings that Diz and Bird made together in the mid-40s are some of the glories of Bebop. Diz & Bird, racing side-by-side, reading each other's minds

Trumpet

b. 10 / 21 / 1917, South Carolina
d. 1 / 6 / 1993, Englewood, New Jersey

Dizzy traveled constantly from the '50s on, often on goodwill tours for America.

by Daryl Long

at breakneck speed, skidding around each corner and laughing at each barely missed wall... .

Eventually Diz and Bird split up. (Opposites attract; then they get sick of each other.) Diz played out the possibilities for big band Bebop. He also mixed Bop with Latin rhythm.

Diz not only had a uniquely athletic sound, he had the look to go with it: his cheeks bulged like Tyson's biceps and the bell of his trumpet bent upward as if by the might of his playing.

They say some nitwit fell on Dizzy's trumpet in 1953 and bent the bell and Diz liked it because "I hear the sound quicker." But we suspect that God bent it upward so He could hear it better.

Diz, the irrepressible clown prince of hip (beret, shades, goatee), always encouraged younger players. He travelled constantly from the 50s on, often on goodwill tours for America. When Diz was in his 70s, he led the United Nations Band (the one with Jeanne Kirkpatrick on drums), reveling in collaborations with Latin Jazz stars (Paquito D'Rivera, sax, and trumpeter Arturo Sandoval).

He was a lifelong campaigner for civil rights, fair treatment of all artists, and for Jazz's acceptance as African-American classical music. In the In the 80s, Diz threatened to run for President—and make Miles the head of the CIA!

Thelonious Monk

Thelonious Sphere Monk is the kind of man you wish they'd done an autopsy on, because there had to be somedamnedthing...? How do you account for somebody that unique? As a child, Monk accompanied his mother when she sang in church. But unless Mrs. Monk was the weirdest singer the world has ever known...little Thelonious Sphere must've somehow dug that music out of his own psyche? (His parents must've had a hunch—I mean, they didn't name him Pat Boone Monk, they named him Thelonious Sphere Monk. What

Pianist and Composer

b. 10 / 10 / 1917, North Carolina
d. 2 / 17 / 1982, New Jersey

Monk played fewer notes per "square inch" of music than any great Jazzman around.

kind of kid could you be expecting to give him a name like Sphere?)

Thelonious Sphere Monk was totally, unselfconsciously certain that what he heard and played was IT, jim. And what he heard and played was so dissonant, so jangly, so full of stops, starts, turns, twists, and sudden silences... . One critic said that Monk's music was "like missing the bottom step in the dark." And if you don't get it, jim, you're the one who needs the shrink, slash, ear doctor. jim. It took the world a while to get it.

Monk is usually listed as one of the original beBoppers. That is and isn't true. Although Monk did play at Minton's with the early beBoppers, his music was different. Bird and Diz's Bop was chord-based, fast and furious music. Although Monk (probably) had as

sophisticated a grasp of harmony as the Boppers, his stop-and-go playing style—and the big "holes" he left in his music—were the dominant features. Monk played fewer notes per "square inch" of music than any great Jazzman around.

Monk played with Coleman Hawkins in 1943. In the late 40s he made some fine recordings of his own compositions. He was falsely imprisoned on drug charges and banned from New York until the mid 50s. Miles Davis helped make Monk's reputation as a composer by frequently playing Monks tunes. Monk's showing in the movie Jazz on a Summer's Day (about the Newport Jazz Festival) really put Monk in the public eye.

Monk the man was like his music: he didn't say much and what he did say was provocative but full of holes. In his last years, he may have gone over the edge into madness, but to be truthful, Monk was so peculiar under normal circumstances that it was hard to tell. In the early 70s, he became very ill and made only one more appearance before his death in 1982.

Monk wore eccentric hats, danced around his piano, and once said to Sonny Rollins: "Man, if there wasn't music in this world, this world wouldn't be shit."

> *In his last years, Monk may have gone over the edge into madness, but to be truthful, he was so peculiar under normal circumstances that it was hard to tell.*

Bud Powell

Piano

b. 9 / 27 / 1924, New York City
d. 8 / 1 / 1966, New York City

Bud Powell was the best of the Bop pianists. Virtually every pianist of the last 40 years has played "in a Bud-Powell-like style" or was "strongly influenced by Bud Powell."

Bud came from a musical family: his father, grandfather, and two brothers were musicians. He spent seven years (age 6-13) studying Bach, Beethoven, Chopin, and Liszt. In his teens, he played in his brother's band and hung out at Minton's, going to school on Monk and the other new geniuses of Bop.

At 18, he recorded with Cootie Williams; at 22, with Charlie Parker. Bud was that good. He always went balls out. By 1949, he was such a brilliant piece of work that Blue Note asked him to record with whomever he chose. (The result was the five-volume The Amazing Bud Powell.)

Sax player Sonny Rollins recalls:

Bud Powell was known in the neighborhood as a sort of mad-genius type. So it was really great in 1949 when he was making this record for Blue Note and he said "Yeah, I want you." I remember on one of those dates I made a mistake on the music and Bud looked over at me.... I mean, he really gave me a look. That was the last time I made that mistake. Though I don't know how I got it together after that look he shot me. He was a very high strung man.

In the early 40s Bud, still a teenager, began showing signs of mental illness. From the late 40s on he was in and out of mental hospitals. In the 50s, his hospital stays grew longer and more frequent and often included mind-numbing electroshock treatment. During the 50s, Powell became an alcoholic and was hostile and abusive to other musicians. In 1959, he moved to Paris, where his wife and friends tried to keep him off of booze and on music. It worked for awhile—he made fine recordings with Danish bassist Niels-Henning Orsted-Pedersen (and with Mingus and Eric Dolphy)—but in 1963 he contracted TB. Jazz musicians played a benefit concert at Birdland (NYC) to help with Bud's medical expenses. He got a little better, returned to the States, and died in a New York hospital in 1966.

Max Roach was the first important modern drummer after Kenny Clarke. Clarke was the pioneer—he ended the predictable rhythm of swing drumming by using the bass drum only for accents and by centering his attention on the top cymbal, where he could give and take accents as he chose. Max Roach took up where Kenny left off. But first a little background.

Max's aunt taught him the piano at the age of eight. He was a drummer in his high school marching band; read music (unusual for a Jazz drummer in the bad ol' days); filled in for three

Drums

b. 1 / 10 / 1924, Brooklyn

Max Roach

nights with Ellington's band (Max was 16 at the time).

Max played for one night with Charlie Parker when he was 18, worked for Coleman Hawkins when he was 19, played with Diz when he was 20, was part of 1945 Diz & Bird quintet and worked for Parker from 1946-49 in the quintet that included Miles Davis.

In the 50s, Max led the best hard Bop group of its time, a quintet featuring the elegant trumpet of Clifford Brown. By that time, Max Roach had taken the drums further than anyone ever thought possible. He used the drums "melodically," played with polyrhythmic looseness, and did little duets with other players. Clifford Brown's tragic death in a car accident left Max Roach (and Jazz) in a state of shock.

Eventually, Max formed a new group with Sonny Rollins that took Jazz drumming into new territory. Max began playing what he called "percussion discussions"—actually, percussion compositions. In the early 60s, Max became political and recorded his Freedom Now Suite. From 1970-76, he refused to permit the release of his records in the U.S., because he felt that black musicians were being exploited. (During that time Max worked as a professor of music at the University of Massachussetts.) In the early 70s, Max began performing with M'Boom Re, an experimental percussion group that makes a point of using Third World percussion instruments.

Bandleader / Bass
Player/ Composer

b. 4 / 22 / 1922, Arizona
d. 1 / 5 / 1979, Mexico

It would be an understatement to say that Jazz's giants have been as ornery a bunch of individualists as you'll find anywhere. Which makes it all the more amazing that even in that crowd, **Charles Mingus** stood out as one ornery sum bitch. Mingus did things his own way. And if people started following him, he did it another way.

Critic Martin Gayford calls Mingus a "chronological misfit." Mingus grew up in the 40s when hip young men were beBoppers. But Mingus not only avoided Bop, he straddled it: his music looked "backwards to Duke Ellington and forwards to free Jazz."

Charles
Mingus

He was a spectacular bass player with a huge tone. He was a composer with great range who gave soloists unprecedented freedom. He was a bandleader who hired some of the most unique musicians ever, from Rahsaan Roland Kirk, who simultaneously played and sang into his flute, to Eric Dolphy, who's brilliant bass clarinet solos (like Monk's piano) often made you feel like you'd stepped into a hole.

A Renaissance Pain in the Ass like Mingus couldn't stop at merely challenging the music—he tilted with the entire music industry as well. Mingus thought that the music industry exploited it's artists—especially its black artists—and that the wrong people made all the money. Of course, he was right on both counts, but Jazz is one skill and making money is another. His independent record labels lost so much money that the demoralized Mingus gave up and even stopped making music in the late 60s. In the early 70s he got a few breaks: He was awarded a Guggenheim fellowship, he cut an album with folk singer Joni Mitchell, and his autobiography (cheerily titled Beneath the Underdog) came out.

Some people mellow out in their last years. Mingus wasn't one of them. He died in 1979, a pain in the ass to the very end. (He's probably down there calling Satan a RedNeck and telling him how to run Hell.)

Sonny Rollins grew up in Brooklyn, studied piano, switched to sax...and 10 years later made a big recording with Bud Powell (1949). In 1950, Rollins worked with Miles Davis, quit in '51, rejoined Miles in '54 to record Oleo—named for one of Rollins' compositions. The Sonny Rollins that emerged on Oleo was an original—unlike the Charlie Parkerized Rollins that preceded him. Rollins left Jazz for a year because of his addiction to drugs. In 1955, Max Roach talked Rollins into coming home, joining up with him and Clifford Brown. It was a wonderful group—then Clifford

Sonny Rollins

died (1956), and everything had to start over.

Whether it was Clifford's death that ignited it or not, one of Rollins' creative peaks started in 1956. What exactly did Rollins do? When all is said and done, Sonny Rollins' claim to fame is that he brilliantly revived "thematic improvisation"—improvisation based on melody, not on chords (like Bop) or modes (simplified scales). Not only did he revive it, but in a tune like "Blue Seven" (Saxophone Colossus, Prestige), Rollins builds his solo with such solid logic that it's almost architectural.

Sonny Rollins is famous for walking around the stage as he plays. He strolls back and forth... . In '59, Rollins strolled away from Jazz for two years. In '68, he spent three years doing Far Eastern philosophy. Have no fear: Rollins is still going strong. Scope out the 1986 documentary film Saxophone Colussus. Like the Terminator, Sonny Rollins always comes back.

Tenor and Soprano Saxophone

b. 9 / 9 / 1930, New York City

> **When all is said and done, Sonny Rollins' claim to fame is that he brilliantly revived "thematic improvision."**

Miles Davis

Trumpet

b. 5 / 26 / 1926, Alton, Ill
d. 9 / 28 / 1991, Santa
Monica, CA

Miles Dewey Davis, son of a St. Louis dentist, took up the trumpet at age 13. His parents nudged him toward classical music, but Miles preferred Jazz. Miles cooled out his parents by enrolling at Julliard in New York but once he got to New York, Miles became obsessed with the music of Charlie Parker. Parker eventually moved in with Miles—and Miles ultimately replaced Dizzy Gillespie in Bird's quintet. Miles, unlike Diz, missed notes and bungled fast tempos. Miles once asked Diz why he couldn't play high and fast like Dizzy. Diz generously replied, "Because you don't hear up there." In a few years, Miles developed his own distinctive sound: low, slow, and moody.

1949 was a big year for Miles: In 1949 he went to Paris and fell head over horn in love with French actress Juliette Greco. During that year, Miles formed his "nonet," featuring laid back arrangements by Gil Evans and saxophonists Gerry Mulligan and Lee Konitz. The group, which made only a few appearances, cut the influential Birth of the Cool album and started "Cool" Jazz.

Miles and Charlie Parker didn't last long as roomies. Miles got rid of Bird but acquired his habit. Miles spent the early 50s being a junkie. Finally, inspired by the humiliating kindness of friends like Max Roach and the discipline of boxing champ Sugar Ray Robinson, Miles broke his addiction to heroin.

He made a comeback at the 1955 Newport Jazz Festival. It gave him enough confidence to form a new band, this time featuring the ferocious John Coltrane. Miles and Trane: Ice and Fire. In the mid-50s, Ice and Fire liberated Jazz from the Cool—which had frozen into a death-mask of inexpressivity. Then, in the late 50s, they cut Kind of Blue—which liberated soloists from the tyranny of chord progressions, changing Jazz forever. Miles, on a creative roll, teamed with Gil Evans' orchestra and together they did Porgy and Bess and Sketches of Spain.

Note: Jazz, judged by its most rigorous standards, nearly demands improvised solos of such singular brilliance that, if they were written out on paper, they would stand up as first rate compositions on their own. Miles, however (especially on his records with Gil Evans), sometimes relies on his sound, which....

Let me put it this way: many people find the voices of certain singers (from Gladys Knight to Pavarotti) so beautiful that they could sing the phone book and you'd buy it. Miles' sound strikes a lot of people like that. (I should know: I'm one of them.) But to some Jazz purists, Miles is often all sound and no substance—just a notch above elevator music.

In 1959, Miles was beaten up and arrested by a white policeman for loitering outside of Birdland, where Miles' combo was headlining.

In the mid-60s, Miles formed a group of young giants (pianist Herbie Hancock, sax Wayne Shorter, bass Ron Carter, drums 16-year-old Tony Williams) that answered "free Jazz" (which Miles found chaotic and meaningless) with his own "structured free Jazz" (my term, not his). Critics tend to be lukewarm about Miles's mid-to-late-60s work. Personally,

> **In the late '50s, Miles' band cut "Kind of Blue" which liberated soloists and changed Jazz forever.**

I consider it some of Miles' (or anybody's) most exciting work. (See, "Is Jazz Dead—Part II" for an Improvisation on that theme.)

In 1969, Miles "fused" Jazz and rock music in the album Bitches Brew. You either loved it or hated it. And if you hated it, you hated everything that came after it. Miles made more Fusion records—none of which were as good as Bitches Brew—until he quit in 1976 (because he "stopped hearing the music"). The great young Jazzmen who had played in his bands went on to form bands of their own.

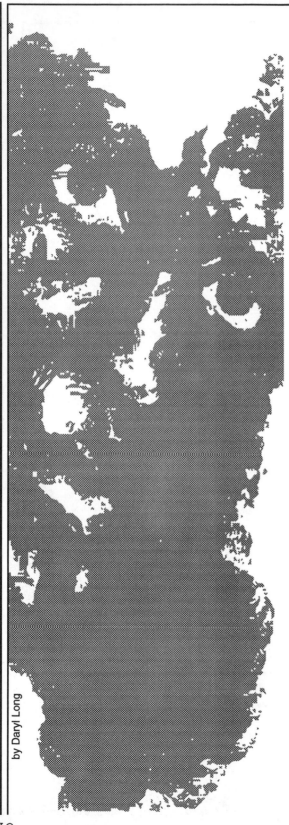

by Daryl Long

Miles made an ill-advised comeback in 1981. Miles, the man—the frog-voiced gremlin from outer space—was more charismatic than ever. But his playing was another story. Miles died in 1991, ten years after his horn.

The bottom line on Miles as far as most critics are concerned, is that ultimately he had a great impact on the Jazz ensemble, but not much on the Jazz solo/improvisation.

Pay no attention to what the critics say;
no statue has ever been put up to a critic.
Attributed to Jean Sibelius—Finnish composer

Pay a little bit of attention to what the critics say—but decide for yourself. And don't measure an artist by how great an impact he has on Jazz, but by how great an impact he has on you.
Attributed to Ron "Sphere" David

I contradict myself?
Very well then I contradict myself.
(I am large, I contain multitudes.)
-- Walt Whitman, Song of Myself

John Coltrane was an R&B sax player, a deeply religious man, a heroin addict, an alcoholic, a shy, world famous, spiritual, commercially successful avant garde Jazz musician.

And that's just scratching the surface. Coltrane's influence on the Jazz of the last 30 years is rivaled by only Miles Davis. Most Jazzmen of Coltrane's stature have been early starters, but Trane

John
Coltrane

was near 30 when he made his rep in the 1955 Miles Davis Quintet. His function in the quintet was to contrast with Miles (as Miles had contrasted with Bird)...but sometimes Trane's obsessive solos were longer than Miles' patience:

"I can't stop playing," he once said to Miles in self-defense.

Miles, who was known to be a trifle irritable on occasion, snap-ped, "Try taking the horn out of your mouth."

In 1957, Coltrane left Miles' group and, shored up by a great religious commitment, quit booze and drugs. Later that year, he played with Monk at the 5 Spot in New York. The long silences in Monk's playing gave Trane plenty of room to explore and expand. In 1959 Coltrane cut Giant Steps, a kind of summing up of his "old" music—and his best album up to that point.

Tenor and Soprano Saxophone

b. 9 / 23 / 1926, N. Carolina
d. 7 / 17 / 1967, New York City

Coltrane's influence on the last 30 years of Jazz is rivaled by only Miles Davis.

In 1960 Trane's recording of "My Favorite Things" was a breakthrough in several ways:

- It uncorked his soprano sax (the first successful use of the instrument since Sidney Bechet).

- It featured the radical new "Modal" style of improvisation.

- It opened the door to Trane's hour-long improvisations (the one on the recording lasted only 13 minutes, but a later live version ran to 45 minutes).

"My Favorite Things" did something even more astonishing: it made Coltrane, a shy, private, uncompromisingly artistic musician, a star outside of Jazz. In 1960, Trane put together his power quartet: Jimmy Garrison on bass, Elvin Jones on drums, and McCoy Tyner on a whole lot of piano. It's beginning to sound like everyone loved Coltrane's music. Nothing could be further from the truth.

Whether you liked his music or not, there was something about the man that was so authentic that nobody doubted his integrity.

Coltrane polarized the hell out of Jazz lovers. To the faithful, half-hour Coltrane solos were mystical experiences; to disbelievers, Coltrane was a mind-numbing bore who didn't play music—all he did was run up and down the scales. Coltrane's 1964 A Love Supreme was more of the same: to enthusiasts, it was the ultimate expression of spirituality; to others—in a way, there were no others—by this point, you either loved him or you didn't listen to his music.

Whether you liked his music or not, there was something about the man that was so authentic that nobody doubted his integrity. In his final phase, Coltrane joined up with youngbloods like Archie Shepp, Albert Ayler, and Pharaoh Sanders for what were, essentially, collective Free Jazz improvisations. Coltrane died of liver cancer in 1967. It wouldn't be far from true to say that Free Jazz was buried with him.

Ornette Coleman played in blues bands in Fort Worth while he was still a teenager, but even then he heard harmony in a way as unique and personal as Van Gogh saw stars. Ornette's music irritated those Texans so much that, on one occasion, they beat the hell out of him and broke his alto sax.

In the late 50s, Ornette wised up and left Texas for California, where he became a beard-and-sandals beatnik. Alas, even in funky California, people generally

Ornette
Coleman

hated his playing—it wasn't uncommon for him to be thrown off bandstands—but eventually he found likeminded souls in trumpeter Don Cherry, bassist Charlie Haden and drummers Ed blackwell and Billy Higgins.

Ornette and the boys practiced together in an L.A. garage, then cut a couple albums—Something Else and Tomorrow is the Question—and split Jazz half-in-two: people from John Lewis (of the Modern Jazz Quartet) to classical composer/conductor Leonard Bernstein thought Ornette was the Second Coming of Bird; blue collar Jazz linebackers like Mingus begged to disagree and attributed Ornette's off-pitch, scramblized music to the fact that, in Mingus's poetic words, "he can't play it straight."

Alto and Tenor Saxophone; Violin and Trumpet

b. 3 / 19 / 1930, Fort Worth, Texas

It was no accident that Ornette won the first ever Guggenheim Fellowship for Jazz.

Ornette didn't give a Texas damn what Mingus thought because his 1960 double quartet (one in each channel) recording, Free Jazz, made his earlier stuff sound like "Jingle Bells."

Critics with perfect hindsight tell us that, although Ornette's music at first seemed contrary to Jazz tradition, if you listen to it four million times it "becomes evident" that Ornette's music is merely an updated version of (or reversion to) early Jazz or Blues.

Sorry, peaches, but I'm not buyin' any of that crap! Ornette was consciously and intentionally playing unmelodic, unrhythmic, unharmonic, unJazz. Unmusic. The reason that intellectuals like John Lewis and tuxedos like Lenny Bernstein liked Ornette was that they understood his intentions. Ornette was playing "Free" Jazz at a time when Jackson Pollock was dripping paint on canvas and John Cage was "composing" by rolling dice to see which note should come next and William Burroughs was "writing" books by scissoring lines out of newspapers and randomly taping them together. Ornette was putting Jazz where the other modern arts were. It was no accident that Ornette won the first ever Guggenheim Fellowship for Jazz!

Ornette was an intellectual who played dumb like Picasso or Miles. Picasso talked like a Greek fortune cookie: You never had any idea what the hell he was talking about. And Miles could be the Prince of Baloney: "Shit, man, I learned more from one of Bird's chords than you could learn from ten years at Julliard."

You can't tell the truth: "Hey, bro, I'd stand on my head and shit nickels if it'd help me come up with something original!"

Music was a continuing adventure to Eric Dolphy. Every solo called for taking new risks and chances.

-- Martin Williams, The Jazz Tradition

Eric Dolphy may be the best kept secret in Jazz. In the words of Lyons & Perlo (JAZZ PORTRAITS): "From 1960 until his death, his presence in a band usually eclipsed even its most illustrious members." A few "illustrious members" that Dolphy eclipsed were Coltrane, Ornette, Mingus... .

Eric
Dolphy

Eric's parents (of West Indian descent) were so supportive that they built a music studio for him in their back yard. Eric studied clarinet and oboe from age seven; in high school he heard Charlie Parker records and switched to alto sax. He won a music scholarship to L.A. City College. His first job was with Roy Porter's band (1948-50); his second was with the Army (1950-52).

Dolphy practiced with whoever'd have him, including Harold Land and the guys from the Clifford Brown-Max Roach band. When Ornette came to town playing his weird shit, most everybody put him down; Dolphy, curious about everything, was fascinated. In 1958, Eric left L.A. with the Chico Hamilton quintet.

In 1960, he moved to New York and looked up Mingus, an old buddy from L.A. Something about Mingus—his passionate compostions, the freedom he gave soloists, plus his thick-headed brilliance as a bass player—brought out the best in Dolphy. At times, he and Mingus actually seem to be conversing (e.g., "What Love," Mingus at

Alto Saxophone / Bass Clarinet / Flute

b. 6 / 20 / 1928, Los Angeles
d. 6 / 29 / 1964, Berlin, W. Germany

Eric Dolphy may be the best kept secret in Jazz.

Antibes, Atlantic; The Charlie Mingus Jazz Workshop: & Stormy Weather, Barnaby—out of print). Dolphy played alto sax, flute, and clarinet...but it was the bass clarinet that put him in a class of his own. (The bass clarinet has a deep, throaty, incredibly resonant sound—when it vibrates, you vibrate —and the contrast between its high and low notes is so radical it makes Dolphy's daredevil jumps seem nearly impossible.)

How to describe Dolphy's playing? Full of leaps, swoops, and wit? A "maximalist" Monk on hormones? Unpredictable to death ...but each surprise is as logical as the killer in a good mystery movie? Dramatic jumps from one end of the horn's register to the other (you're having a normal conversaton...all of a sudden you're talking to his feet).

Critics love to compare Dolphy to Coltrane and Ornette. Martin Gayford finds Dolphy "'Less messianic than Coltrane" and "less drastically radical than Ornette." (I can get next to that.) Dolphy played on Ornette's famous Free Jazz (Atlantic, 1960). Dolphy and Coltrane played together off and on between 1961-63. Not only were they both obsessed with music, they were both health-food nuts. Eric was a diabetic, and Trane wanted to undo the harm done by drugs and booze—so they used to sit around rapping about music and munching on seeds and nuts.

> **Dolphy was in great demand as a soloist, leader, and composer, practicing hard to revolutionize the flute.**

By 1964, Dolphy was in great demand as a soloist, leader, and composer. He was practicing hard to revolutionize the flute. He was touring Europe because they loved his music...then he died. Diabetes. 36 years old. Just like that.

Betty Carter

Betty Carter is something special. In high-school she invented ways of recreating Diz and Bird's solos with her voice. She debuted as a singer at 17, backed by Dizzy's band! From 1948-51, she sang with Lionel Hampton—who fired her half a dozen times because she admitted she preferred Bop to Swing.

Vocalist

b. 5 / 16 / 1930, Flint, MI

She eventually quit and went to New York, where she sang with people like Max Roach, Charlie Parker, and Miles. In the late '50s, she went on tour with Ray Charles. Ray, who knew the real thing baybaayy, when he saw it (whoops)—when he heard it—communicated his enthusiasm so effectively that major record houses began courting Ms. Carter, trying to con—persuade —her to forget that beBop crap and manufacture some nice hit tunes.

Betty Carter did what other musicians of every class, color, and shoe size only dream of doing: She told them to piss off and started her own record company—Bet-Car—in 1969.

At the risk of having the Jazz Police kick in my door, I confess that in my opinion Betty Carter is the best Jazz singer ever. She has great voices (at least two of them), scats like it's an art (not a curiousity), phrases, improvises, and trades riffs like a horn player, composes smart new songs, resurrects dumb old ones, sings faster and slower than anyone around...and she's fun!

There's more: Since the early 1980s, she's made a point of recording and promoting artists who've been ignored by the big record companies. (Betty Carter is my idea of a hero.)

If **Keith Jarrett** had died at age 30, he'd be considered one of the great Jazz pianists of all time, but the inconsiderate rascal is still alive, so the line on his playing has become approximately: "He's great at something, but it isn't Jazz."
Keith Jarrett wasn't a child prodigy, he was an infant prodigy. He was playing music at age three. When he was seven, he gave recitals

Keith
Jarrett

of classical music and his own compositions. He studied classical music, toured with Fred Waring's orchestra, studied Jazz at Berklee

Piano

b. 5 / 8 / 1945, Pennsylvania

College of Music in Boston, moved to Harlem, played with Art Blakey's Jazz Messengers for a year, then quit Blakey's hard Bop group to join the Charles Lloyd Quartet. By then, Jarrett had reached the ripe old age of 21.

Jarrett was playing music at age three and gave recitals of classical music and his own compositions by age seven.

In the Lloyd Quartet's dramatic, romanticized style, Jarrett flowered. His rhapsodic, soulful solos were often the high point of the band's performances.
Jarrett was known for his singing, lyrical improvisations, spiced with more than a hint of the gospel-tinged tradition.
Nor was he afraid to be unconventional, strumming on the piano's strings...
from JAZZ PORTRAITS by Len Lyons & Don Perlo.

In 1969, Keith left the Lloyd Quartet to form his own group—and to work with Miles' seminal Fusion groups. In no time at all, he alienated the "fusers" by denouncing electric instruments as a crutch. In 1972, Jarrett formed a group with two Ornette Coleman alumni—Dewey Redman (sax) and Charlie Haydn (bass)—and drummer Paul Motian. The group recorded over a dozen albums and played everything from hard Bop to Free Jazz.

In the mid 70s, Jarrett made a series of solo piano records for ECM (Germany)—mainly of live concerts.

Jarrett's solo style was unprecedented, combining a European, pulselike beat with melodic excursions that oscillated between ecstatic romanticism and soulful blues.

Jarrett's performances were totally spontaneous and he emphatically asserted that he had no idea what he would be playing until he sat down at the piano bench.
from JAZZ PORTRAITS by Len Lyons & Don Perlo

..if Liszt had been born in the same time and place, this is how he would play.
from JAZZ by John Fordham

(Yes, classical composer/pianist Franz Liszt was a great improviser. There isn't much difference between Jazz and classical music.)

Jarrett's solo concerts—which might go from gospel to Jazz to classical to country in a heartbeat—were confusing enough for some Jazz fans, but when Keith composed a few note-for-note, no-improvisation pieces for orchestra/chamber groups, many straight arrow Jazz lovers thought he'd gone too far. (Don't

kid yourself: Jazz has its own version of Political Correctness.) So, since Keith wasn't considerate enough to die for his sins, the Jazz Police have banished him from the pantheon of Jazz greats.

If Jazz isn't big enough
to include Keith Jarrett,
it's Jazz's loss.

Discography

THE CANON:

There's been a lot of fuss in recent years over the "canon." The canon refers to a list of books that make up the "indispensible basics of a culture." The classics.

Multiculturalists and feminists argue that the canon consists of a bunch of DWEMs—Dead White European Males. They're right.

Most people haven't noticed, but Jazz also has a canon— the Discography—the "indispensible classics" of Jazz. However...instead of DWEMs, Jazz's canon consists of DBAAMs— Dead Black African American Males.

New Orleans around 1900

Scott Joplin
Scott Joplin—1916
Biograph, 1916

Jelly Roll Morton
The Saga of Mr. Jelly Lord
Circle, 1938

Fats Waller
Fractious Fingering
RCA Victor, 1929-36

The Original Dixieland Jazz Band
The Original Dixieland Jazz Band
RCA Victor, 1917-36

King Oliver's Jazz Band
The Complete 1923 OKEHs
EMI, 1923

Louis Armstrong
Louis Armstrong & Earl Hines
Philips, 1928

Sidney Bechet
The Bluebird Sessions
Bluebird, 1932-43

Masterpiece

Louis Armstrong
The Hot Fives & Sevens
Okeh, 1925-28

Chicago, New York, Swing

Earl Hines & his Orchestra
Swinging in Chicago
Coral, 1934-35

Bix Beiderbecke
The Bix Beiderbecke Story
Philips, 1927-29

Various Artists
Chicago Jazz
Coral, 1939-40
Featuring: Eddie Condon & his Chicagoans; Jimmy McPartland & his orchestra; George Wettling's Chicago Rhythm Kings.

Landmark Recordings

Benny Goodman
Carnegie Hall Jazz Concert
Philips, 1938

Coleman Hawkins All Stars
Coleman Hawkins All Stars
HMV, 1935-46

Duke Ellington & his Orchestra
At His Very Best
RCA, 1927-46

Count Basie & his Orchestra
Jumpin' at the Woodside
Ace of Hearts, 1937-39

Duke Ellington
Ellington at Newport
CBS, 1956

BeBop—Giving Swing the Finger

Art Tatum
Solo Masterpieces
Pablo, 1953-54

Charlie Parker
Bird Lives—The Complete Dial Masters
Spotlite, 1946-47

> **Charlie Parker**
> *Bird: The Savoy Recordings*
> Savoy, 1944-48
> Featuring: Dizzy Gillespie, Miles Davis, Bud Powell, John Lewis,, Duke Jordan, Max Roach.

Bud Powell
The Amazing Bud Powell
Blue Note, 1949-53

Thelonious Monk
The Blue Note Sessions
Blue Note, 1947-52

Dizzy Gillespie and his Orchestra
Old Man Rebop
HMV, 1946-49

The Quintet
Jazz at Massey Hall
Debut, 1953
Featuring: Bird, Diz, Bud Powell, Charles Mingus, Max Roach!

Birth (and death) of the Cool

The COOL:

Miles Davis
Birth of the Cool
Capitol, 1949-50

Gerry Mulligan & Chet Baker
Mulligan/Baker
Prestige, 1951, 52, 65

The Modern Jazz Quartet
One Never Knows
Atlantic, 1957

The Dave Brubeck Quartet
Time Out
CBS, 1959

HARD BOP:

Clifford Brown & Max Roach
At Basin Street
Mercury, 1956

Sonny Rollins
Saxophone Colossus
Prestige, 1956

Miles Davis
Workin' with the Miles Davis Quintet
Prestige, 1956

John Coltrane
Giant Steps
Atlantic, 1959

FUNK:

The Cannonball Adderly Quintet
Mercy, Mercy, Mercy!
Captitol, 1967

Lee Morgan
The Sidewinder
Blue Note, 1964

Intermission: The Jazz Singers

Ma Rainey & others
Ma Rainey & the Classic Blues Singers
CBS, 1920-39
With: Ma Rainey, Mamie Smith, Clara Smith, Bessie Smith, & others.

Bessie Smith
The Bessie Smith Story, Vol. 3
CBS, 1925-27

Billie Holiday
The Golden Years, Vol. 2
CBS, 1937-38

Billie Holiday
Lady in Satin
CBS, 1958

Ella Fitzgerald
Ella Fitzgerald, Vol. 1
Classics, 1935-41

Sarah Vaughn
Sassy Sings
SAGA, 1946-47

Anita O'Day
Travelin' Light
World, 1961

Leon Thomas
Spirits Known and Unknown
Flying Dutchman, 1969

Betty Carter
Look What I Got
PolyGram, 1988

Cassandra Wilson
Blue Skies
JMT, 1988

From Kind of Blue to Avant-Garde

Sun Ra
Angels & Demons at Play
Saturn, 1955-57

The Charlie Mingus Jazz Workshop
Pithecanthropus Erectus
Atlantic, 1956

Miles Davis
Kind of Blue
CBS, 1959
With: Coltrane, Cannonball Adderly, Wynton Kelly, Bill Evans, Paul Chambers, J. Cobb

Ornette Coleman
The Shape of Jazz to Come
Atlantic, 1959

John Coltrane
My Favorite Things
Atlantic, 1960
With: McCoy Tyner, Steve Davis, Elvin Jones.

Miles Davis
Sketches of Spain
CBS, 1959

Charles Mingus
The Black Saint and the Sinner Lady
Impulse, 1963

Herbie Hancock
Maiden Voyage
Blue Note, 1965
Featuring: Hancock, Freddie Hubbard, George Coleman, Ron Carter, Tony Williams.

Eric Dolphy
Out to Lunch
Blue Note, 1964

John Coltrane
Ascension
Impulse, 1965

McCoy Tyner
The Real McCoy
Blue Note, 1967
Featuring: Joe Henderson,
Ron Carter, Elvin Jones.

Carla Bley
Escalator over the Hill
JCOA/Virgin, 1968-71

Fusion (and CONfusion) in the 1970s

Miles Davis
Bitches Brew
CBS, 1969

The Mahavishnu Orchestra
The Inner Mounting Flame
CBS, 1971

Weather Report
I Sing the Body Electric
CBS, 1971-72

Keith Jarrett
Koln Concert
ECM, 1975

The 80s/90s—HipHop & Young Fogeys

Art Blakey and the Jazz Messengers
Keystone 3
Concord, 1982
Featuring: the Marsalis
brothers.

Greg Osby
Season of Renewal
JMT, 1989

Steve Coleman and Five Elements
On the Edge of Tomorrow
JMT, 1986

Keith Jarrett/Gary Peacock/Jack DeJohnette
Standards Live
ECM, 1985

Joe Henderson
The State of the Tenor
Blue Note, 1985

Geri Allen
Etudes
Soul Note, 1987

Tony Williams
Angel Street
Blue Note, 1988
Featuring: Williams, Wallace
Roney, Billy Pierce, Mulgrew
Miller, Charnett Moffet.

Listening to the World

Dollar Brand [now **Abdullah Ibrahim**]
African Space Program
Enja, 1973
Note: South African composer/pianist, with American avant gardists (John Stubblefield, Hamiet Bluiett, Sonny Fortune).

Mike Gibbs
The Only Chrome Waterfall Orchestra
Bronze, 1975
Note: Zimbabwe-born keyboard player & composer.

Vagif Mustafa-Zadeh
Aspiration
East Wind Records, 1978
Note: Azerbaidjani pianist, blending Islamic folk music with Bill Evans-like piano.

Zakir Hussainn
Making Music
ECM, 1986
Note: Indian (Parker-influenced) tabla player; & John McLaughlin

Toshiko Akiyoshi
Interlude
Concord, 1987
Note: Japan's top Jazz pianist.

Rabih Abou-Khalil
NAFAS
ECM, 1988
Note: Jazz on Lebanese oud and bamboo flute. (It's for real.)

Barbara Dennerlein
Hot Stuff
Enja, 1990
Note: German organist.

John Surman
Road to Saint Ives
ECM, 1990
Note: British bass clarinet, soprano & baritone sax

Salif Keita
Amen
Mango, 1991
Note: Keita, spectacular singer from Mali, joins forces with West African and Carribean musicians, plus the supersaxes of Wayne Shorter; Joe Zawinul, keyboards; Carlos Santana, guitar.

Courtney Pine
To the Eyes of Creation
Island, 1992
Note: British sax—just turned 30!

Glossary

arrangement (or chart): The written adaptation of a composition for a particular group of instruments.

attack: The act or style of initiating a sound on an instrument.

backbeats: The second and fourth beats in a four-beat measure. European classical music emphasizes beats one and three; Jazz usually accents the back or "after" beats.

ballad: A slow song, usually with lyrics that tell a story.

Bebop (or Bop): The first modern Jazz style; evolved in the 40s. Bop's emphasis was on complexity, harmonic improvisation, and technical virtuosity. Spectacular examples: Charlie Parker and Dizzy Gillespie.

Blues: A 12-bar song form that evolved from black spirituals and work songs. It's unique elements are blue notes, speechlike inflection, and emotional expression.

brass: In a big band, the trumpet and trombone sections (which may also include French horn, tuba, etc.

call-and-response: In a Jazz group setting, it is the alternation of a solo statement with an ensemble reply. Historically, its evolution can be traced back to Africa and to British church service. Its clearest non-musical "relative" is the "dialogue" between the congregation and the minister in African American church services.

chord: Three or more notes played simultaneously (as on a piano) that outline a scale.

chord changes (or changes): The sequence of chords that provides the harmonic structore of a composition.

Cool Jazz: A small-group Jazz style that originated in the 1950s with Miles Davis' Birth of the Cool, and is often identified with "West Coast Jazz." Its main features are subdued expression and a more intellectual approach.

counterpoint: Two or more melodies (each strong enough to stand alone) played simultaneously to produce a single musical fabric.

cross-rhythm: A rhythm that conflicts with the original rhythm.

Dixieland: A general label that usually refers to early New Orleans style Jazz or to the version of (pre-1930s) Chicago Jazz played by white musicians.

Free Jazz (also Avant-Garde Jazz or the new thing): A controversial style of Jazz that emerged in the 1960s in the music of Ornette Coleman, Cecil Taylor and others. The music—"free" of either conventional rhythm, harmony, melody, or all-of-the-above—often strikes new listeners as chaotic and UNmusical.

front line: A group's main soloists, usually horn players.

Funk: A Jazz style that combined modern Jazz with earlier black music styles, especially Gospel and Blues. Notable examples: Horace Silver, Bobby Timmons, and (sometimes) Cannonball Adderly.

Fusion: A mix of different musical styles—especially Jazz & Rock or Jazz & R&B.

Hard Bop: A 1950s Jazz style that emerged as a reaction to the stiflingly lack of emotion of Cool Jazz. Notable examples: Mid-50s Miles Davis and Art Blakey's Jazz Messengers.

improvisation: An on-the-spot musical "mini-composition" in which a player (or, less often, a group) deviates from the original theme (or song or tune) with as much ingenuity as he/she can manage without abandoning the original theme.

Although improvisation is not necessarily essential to Jazz, it is one of Jazz's central elements and greatest challenges. It's what separates the great players from the merely good ones.

jam session: An informal performance by musicians who usually don't play together—usually for the pure joy of it!

Jazz: The shortest definition of Jazz I can come up with is this entire book. What I have not given you so far is Jazz's etymology (the origin of the word; where it came from).

"The word 'jazz' is probably creolized Ki-Kongo: it is similar in sound and original meaning to 'jizz,' the American vernacular for semen."
—Robert Farris Thompson
Flash of the Spirit: African & Afro-American Art & Philosophy

Modal Jazz: A style of Jazz based on modes (types of scales) instead of chord changes that freed Jazz musicians from the constraints of Bop. Notable examples: Miles Davis' Kind of Blue and John Coltrane's My Favorite Things.

obbligato: A razzle-dazzle countermelody, played "behind" the soloist, often for great effect. Notable example: New Orleans clarinet doing pretty little things behind the cornet solos. Spectacular example: Lester Young's saxophone dancing behind Billie Holiday's vocals.

polyrhythm: Two or more rhythms played at the same time.

Ragtime: A "pre-Jazz" hybrid that combined European harmonies with the syncopated rhythms of black folk music. Most notable example: Scott Joplin.

riff: A simple musical phrase that's traded back and forth by soloists in small group Jazz (usually spontaneous) or by (brass or wind) "sections" in big band Jazz (usually prewritten).

scale: A series of notes arranged in ascending or descending order.

scat singing: A vocal style in which the singer essentially becomes an instrumentalist by using nonsense syllables instead of words. The singer, deprived of the "safety net" of a song's lyrics, has to "play" a solo that "holds together" on purely musical terms.

stride: A post-Ragtime piano style (in which the left hand alternately plays bass notes and chords) rhythmically looser and more improvisational than Ragtime. Early exponents: James P. Johnson & Willie "The Lion" Smith. Later version: Count Basie.

Swing (the noun): Dance-oriented big-band music that became immensely popular during the 1930s. Notable examples: Benny Goodman, Count Basie, Duke Ellington.

swing (the verb): A feeling of rhythmic urgency and drive, caused (according to our best estimates) by playing different rhythms at the same time—a centuries-old characteristic of much African music. It is swing—the verb—that makes a great Jazz soloist like Louis Armstrong sound like an entire orchestra!

syncopation: A distinctive approach to rhythm In which one part (or, on a piano, one hand) plays the strong beats and the other part accents the backbeats. It's syncopation, more than anything, that makes Ragtime so bouncy.

Third Stream: Narrow Definition: Fusion of Classical compositional forms and orchestras with Jazz improvisation, soloists, and swing (the verb). (Notable example: Gunther Schuller, a classical dude who is crazy for Jazz, is the Father, Son, and Holy Ghost of the movement.)

Broad Definition: Any music that fuses Jazz with Classical music. (Notable example: The Modern Jazz Quartet.)

The Basics

Some things are so basic that become invisible: Introductions to Jazz almost never mention them, and even a conscientious dude whose name I won't mention finds himself at the end of this book before I realize that I have not answered the most basic and important question about actually listening to Jazz:

What, in the most basic sense, goes on in a Jazz performance?

Do they play songs? Are they just playing what they feel like playing when they feel like playing it? Is there any pattern? Do they follow any "rules"? Or...

This, in the most basic sense, is what's going on in 90% of the Jazz, live or recorded, anywhere ever (and I'm amazed at how many long-time listeners don't know it):

Virtually every "number" (whether it's a pop song, an original composition, or a rip-off of Beethoven) in virtually every Jazz performance, live or recorded, follows this pattern:

1. **The entire Group states the theme (they play the song)**
2. **Then the players, one at a time, take turns playing a solo**
3. **After all the solos are finished, the entire Group restates the theme (they play the song again).**

...end of Song #1...

Recommended Reading

Bechet, Sidney. *Treat It Gentle.*

Crow, Bill. *Jazz Anecdotes.* New York-Oxford; Oxford University Press, 1990.

Feather, Leonard. *The Encyclopedia of Jazz.* New York; Horizon Press, 1960.

Fordham, John. *Jazz.* New York; Dorling Kindersly, Inc, 1993.

Gayford, Martin. *JAZZ—the essential CD guide.* San Francisco, CA; Collins Publishers, 1993.

Hentoff, Nat. *Jazz Is.* New York; Limelight Editions, 1991.

Jones, LeRoi. *Blues People.* New York; William Morrow and Company, 1963.

Long, Daryl. *Miles Davis for Beginners.* New York; Writers and Readers Publishing, Inc. 1992.

Lyons, Len & Perlo, Don. *Jazz Portraits.* New York; William Morrow and Company, 1989.

McRae, Barry. *The Jazz Handbook.* Boston; G.K. Hall & Co., 1987.

Rowland, Mark & Scherman, Tony, editors. *The Jazz Musician: 15 years of interviews.* New York; St. Martin's Press, 1994.

Sidran, Ben. *Talking Jazz.* Petaluma, CA; Pomegranate Artbooks, 1992.

Thompson, Robert Farris. *Flash of the Spirit.* New York; Random House, 1983.

Troupe, Quincy. *Miles: The Autobiography.* New York; Simon & Schuster, 1989.

Williams, Martin. *The Jazz Tradition.* New York-Oxford; Oxford University Press, 1993 [2nd edition].

Index